Beginning
Family Law

Whether you're new to higher education, coming to legal study for the first time or just wondering what Family Law is all about, **Beginning Family Law** is the ideal introduction to help you hit the ground running. Starting with the basics and an overview of each topic, it will help you come to terms with the structure, themes and issues of the subject so that you can begin your Family Law module with confidence.

Adopting a clear and simple approach with legal vocabulary carefully clarified, Jonathan Herring breaks the subject of family law down using practical everyday examples to make it understandable for anyone, whatever their background. Diagrams and flowcharts simplify complex issues, important cases are identified and explained and on-the-spot questions help you recognise potential issues or debates within the law so that you can contribute in classes with confidence.

Beginning Family Law is an ideal first introduction to the subject for LLB, GDL or ILEX students and especially international students, those enrolled on distance learning courses or on other degree programmes.

Jonathan Herring is a Tutor and Fellow in Law at Exeter College, Oxford. His research interests lie in criminal law, family law and medical law and he is the author of a number of best-selling textbooks across these areas.

Beginning the Law

A new introductory series designed to help you master the basics and progress with confidence.

Beginning Constitutional Law, Nick Howard
Beginning Contract Law, Nicola Monaghan and Chris Monaghan
Beginning Criminal Law, Claudia Carr and Maureen Johnson
Beginning Equity and Trusts, Mohamed Ramjohn
Beginning Employment Law, James Marson
Beginning Evidence, Chanjit Singh Landa
Beginning Family Law, Jonathan Herring
Beginning Human Rights, Howard Davis

Following in Spring 2015

Beginning Business Law, Chris Monaghan
Beginning Land Law, Sarah King
Beginning Medical Law, Claudia Carr

www.routledge.com/cw/beginningthelaw

Beginning
Family Law

JONATHAN HERRING

Routledge
Taylor & Francis Group

LONDON AND NEW YORK

First published 2015
by Routledge
2 Park Square, Milton Park, Abingdon, Oxon OX14 4RN

and by Routledge
711 Third Avenue, New York, NY 10017

Routledge is an imprint of the Taylor & Francis Group, an informa business

British Library Cataloguing in Publication Data
A catalogue record for this book is available from the British Library

Library of Congress Cataloging in Publication Data
Herring, Jonathan, author.
    Beginning family law/Professor Jonathan Herring.
    pages cm. – (Beginning the law)
    Includes bibliographical references and index.
    1. Domestic relations – Great Britain. I. Title.
    KD750.H465 2015
    346.4101'5 – dc23
    2014028354

ISBN: 978-1-138-77862-7 (hbk)
ISBN: 978-1-138-77861-0 (pbk)
ISBN: 978-1-315-77179-3 (ebk)

Typeset in Vectora
by Florence Production Ltd, Stoodleigh, Devon, UK

Contents

Table of Cases

Table of Legislation

Guide to the Companion Website

www.routledge.com/cw/beginningthelaw

Visit the *Beginning the Law* website to discover a comprehensive range of resources designed to enhance your learning experience.

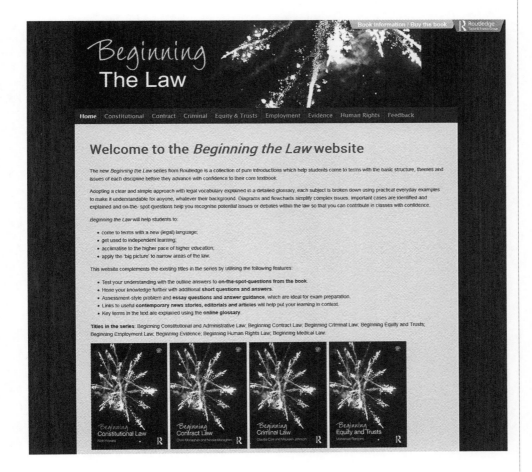

Answers to on-the-spot questions
The author's suggested answers to the questions posed in the book.

Online glossary
Reinforce your legal vocabulary with our online glossary. You can find easy to remember definitions of all key terms, listed by chapter for each title in the *Beginning the Law* series.

Chapter 1
An introduction to family law

For most people their relationships and their families are the most important part of their lives. Nothing can bring greater joy than a happy relationship. Few things can bring greater misery than a relationship that goes wrong. Family law, therefore, deals with hallowed ground; the most sensitive issues in people's lives. It is not surprising then it is highly controversial and raises issues of considerable significance.

This book will seek to introduce you to the fascinating world of family law. On its own, it will not provide you with enough information to get a first in your final exams! However, it will start you down the road to doing really well in your work on this topic. The book provides you with an introduction to the key legal principles; the main cases and important pieces of statute that you need for family law. It will lay the foundation for a successful study of family law.

One of the joys about family law is that generally the facts of the cases are easy to understand. The cases do not involve complex financial arrangements you have never heard of, or dense corporate structures that make no sense. Rather we are entering the world of love, heartbreak and the chaos of human relationships. That makes the cases more interesting! It makes it easier to get a handle on the subject and therefore to do well.

THE STRUCTURE OF THE BOOK

We start, in Chapter 2, with marriage and civil partnership. As we shall see, marriage has long been regarded as at the heart of family law, but that idea is increasingly coming under challenge. Many couples choose to live together outside marriage. Even for those who do marry, the precise meaning of marriage is unclear. As the debates over same-sex marriage demonstrate, there is considerable uncertainty over the extent to which marriage is a religious, patriarchal or individual institution. Chapter 3 turns to cohabitation, a popular form of relationship for many couples. It gives them freedom to enter or leave without involving courts. But with that freedom comes considerable problems. It means a person can suffer serious financial disadvantage as a result of a relationship, but receive no compensation from the other person. A cohabitant, under the current law, is taking a huge financial risk in deciding not to get married.

In Chapter 4 we discuss divorce. Traditionally the law has sought to uphold marriage by only allowing divorce where something has gone seriously wrong in the marriage. Divorce law has moved on. It is now recognised that by the time people seek a divorce, any hope of saving the marriage has passed. Indeed the question is now regularly asked, if a couple recognise that their marriage has come to an end, should the law do any more than give them what they want? Telling the couple that their relationship is not "that bad" and they should stay together seems very paternalistic. As we shall see there is even a suggestion that divorce should become "on demand" through a computer programme.

In Chapter 5 we turn to a common cause of divorce: domestic abuse. This difficult but extremely important issue has troubled family lawyers for decades. In the past it was dismissed as a private matter, best left to the parties to resolve themselves. Now it is recognised as a major social problem and it has attracted considerable attention. There is still much work to be done to find an effective response.

Chapter 6 looks at the issues relating to finance on separation. It is now common to read in the papers of wives of millionaires receiving extraordinary sums of money on divorce. This chapter will try and explain the thinking the courts use when producing these results. However, the chapter will also emphasise that for most people divorce produces poverty, especially for women. It is not always the windfall the media sometimes portrays it to be.

So far you might be forgiven for thinking we have forgotten the most important people in family law; the children. Don't worry – the rest of the book will focus on them. Chapter 7 looks at the definition of parent. How do we decide who will be given the status of parenthood and the authority to make decisions in relation to a child. In the past the question "Who is the parent of this child?" was relatively straightforward. But in this age of sperm donor, multiple family breakdown and same-sex parents, the issue has become far more complex.

Chapter 8 looks at the position of children's rights. To what extent should children be able to make decisions for themselves? Is it best to choose an age at which children are deemed mature enough to make decisions or should we test children to see how intelligent and sensible they are? How can we balance the rights of parents to make decisions about children with giving respect to children?

Chapter 9 looks at the issue of child abuse. How serious does abuse have to be before a child can be removed from their parents? Some have suggested that we need to recognise that not every child can have a perfect parent and so we have to be tolerant of a wide range of parental qualities and only remove children when there is appalling abuse. But does that protect children adequately? And what are we to do in cases where there are suspicions that children are being abused but there is no clear evidence to prove it? These are enormously difficult questions and give rise to some of the most troubling cases in family law.

Chapter 10 looks at the question of adoption. What needs to be shown before a child can be adopted? What should the relationship be between an adopted child and her birth family? We will also look at the concept of special guardianship, which provides a long term carer for a child, without severing completely the links between the child and the birth family.

READING FAMILY LAW CASES

Most people study family law in their second or third year when you will be familiar with how to read a case generally, so this section will focus on the particular issues that are raised in relation to reading family law cases. The first point to note is that the facts of the cases can be really interesting! Indeed there is a danger that you will get so caught up reading the facts that you will lose sight of the key legal points. It is understandable if the case is emotionally engaging, but do not let this prevent you from making an intellectual assessment of the decision.

A second point is that many family law cases depend on their particular facts. A case on a dispute over children may tell you about how the court decided to resolve the dispute for that particular child in that particular family. Rarely do family law cases establish rules that you can automatically apply in a particular case. Most family law cases are used in exams in one of two ways. First, it might be used as an example of the tensions the law has to deal with and how the law needs to balance competing interests. Second, it might illustrate one factor that can be used in deciding a case. So, you might not in a problem question be able to use a case to establish a rule. For example, you might say in a criminal law exam: "In the case of *R v Cunningham* the Court of Appeal established that the mens rea for murder is an intention to kill or cause grievous bodily harm." In many contexts in family law you cannot use a case in that way. In a family law problem question it is more likely you would say: "One factor the court will take into account is the fact that generally it is seen as good that a child keeps contact with both parents; see, for example, *Re W (Children)*."

A third point is that family courts tend to be very aware that in many cases a range of acceptable results might be taken. If the appeal court is persuaded that a judge took into account all the relevant factors and produced a reasonable conclusion it will uphold the judgement, even though the court itself might have reached a different conclusion. Your answer in an exam might, therefore, quite properly refer to a range of orders that a judge might sensibly make. In short, in family law, there is often not a clear right or wrong answer.

STATUTES

Statutes play a part in family law as they do in nearly all areas of law. However, statutes in family law tend to be slightly different from other areas of law. For example, the Theft Act 1968 defines the offence of theft. It lists the five elements that need to be proved and explains what those elements mean. In family law a statute will often state a general principle and list factors that can be taken into account. For example, s 1(1) of the Children Act 1989 states that in resolving disputes over the upbringing of a child, the child's welfare should be the court's paramount concern, although it then, in s 1(3), provides a long list of factors that should be taken into account in deciding what is or is not in a child's welfare. The statute does not, however, seek to define what welfare actually is.

This means that in a problem question in an exam it is not possible to give a definitive answer as to what order a court can make. You should go through each of the statutory factors and explain how either side might want to rely on that factor. Although you cannot say for sure what a court will order, it is a good idea to indicate how you think the factors will be weighed.

FAMILY LAW ESSAY QUESTIONS

Essay questions in family law typically ask you to consider not only what the law is, but also the theoretical issues surrounding the law. You will need, therefore, to learn not only what the law is, but also why it is the way it is; what social changes have influenced the law; and what broader policy issues are at play.

One trap, however, that some students fall into is getting carried away by the emotions in a particular issue. Let us say, for example, there was a question on same-sex marriage. That may be an issue on which you have strong views. Beware of writing an answer that might work well as a *Guardian* or *Daily Mail* editorial (depending on your point of view), but that does not demonstrate to the examiner you are aware of the legal issues or the law. You should never write an essay that fails to mention a single case or a statute. While you need not shy away from making an argument, it should be rooted in a clear demonstration to the examiner that you understand the law, the leading cases and the important statutory principles.

A good answer will show knowledge not only of the case law and statute but also the academic arguments. Citing the views of academics and discussing them will prevent your answers becoming too "journalistic" and show the examiner your have read the material you have been set.

FAMILY LAW PROBLEM QUESTIONS

Many universities use problem questions in an examination. You will already be familiar with these and have developed techniques to respond to them. There are, however, a number of issues that are particular to family law problems.

The first is that in many cases there is no "right answer". The best you can do is to list the factors a court will take into account. You might predict what outcome the court could make, but you will want to make it clear that there is considerable judicial discretion in this area.

The second, flowing from the above, is that in many cases you can use the statutory framework to guide your answer. For example, in deciding what order to make in relation to financial issues on divorce, Matrimonial Causes Act 1973, s 25 lists nine factors that will be taken into account. You can go through each of these one by one. Cases can be referred to where the courts have placed particular weight on that factor or which have explained how it is relevant. Remember to not just list the factors but to apply them to the factors of the case. So do not just say "the age of the parties is a factor to take into account", but rather say, for example, "the fact that Angela is 68 is relevant because she cannot reasonably be expected to find full-time employment at this point in her life and will be entering retirement. This means she will need income from her husband to support her in the future."

HELPFUL JOURNALS

Family Law provides some helpful summaries of cases and good short articles. It also carries up-to-date news on family law.

Child and Family Law Quarterly provides some excellent articles and detailed case comments.

Journal of Social Welfare and Family Law has some good articles on a broad range of issues relating to families.

International Journal of Law, Policy and Family has some fascinating articles on family law, often from an international perspective.

SOME HELPFUL WEBSITES

There are some excellent family law blogs including:

www.marilynstowe.co.uk/

www.pinktape.co.uk/

http://flwblog.lawweek.co.uk/

The following provides up-to-date news on family law:

www.familylawweek.co.uk/site.aspx?i=ho0

Chapter 2
Marriage and civil partnership

LEARNING OBJECTIVES

After reading this chapter you should be able to:

- understand the nature of marriage;
- explain when a marriage is void or voidable;
- appreciate the differences between marriage and civil partnership.

INTRODUCTION

This chapter will explore who can marry whom and the significance of **marriage**. It will include a discussion of the grounds on which a marriage can be **void** or **voidable**. It will also explore the introduction of same-sex marriage and the status of **civil partnership**.

Marriage has traditionally been at the heart of family law. However, it has come under challenge in recent years. First, there have been extensive debates over who can marry. In particular, there have been fierce debates over whether marriage should be permitted for same-sex couples. We now have the Marriage (Same-Sex Couples) Act 2013, which has removed the bar on marriages for same-sex couples. Second, we have seen a steady decrease in the number of couples choosing to marry. Nowadays half of all children are born to couples who are not married. Marriage can no longer be assumed to be the natural status for those raising children or wanting to live together. Third, there have been persistent complaints that marriage is outdated, in upholding sexist assumptions about husbands, wives and sexual morality. Marriage is to some extent under threat. Nevertheless, surveys indicate that marriage is still popular as an ideal. Most people want to get married, even if they are not sure they will ever find the right person!

REAL WORLD

There were 247,890 marriages in 2011. That is dramatically fewer than the 480,300 in 1972. For each 1,000 adult women 19.8 were married in 2001. The equivalent figure for men was 22. These are a decrease from 2000 when the figures were 25.7 and 29.5.

In 2011 70 per cent of marriages were civil ceremonies (i.e. not religious ones). This indicates that it is not true that marriage is restricted to religious observers.

Notably in 2010 34 per cent of marriages involved at least one party who had been married before. This suggests that there are people marrying several times and they are keeping the numbers up.

VOID MARRIAGE

It is the law on void marriages that sets out who can marry. If a marriage is void then there is no legal marriage. Section 11 of the Matrimonial Causes Act 1973 states which marriages are void, namely those where:

- either of the parties is under the age of 16;
- either of the parties is married to someone else;
- the parties are within the degrees of prohibited relationship (e.g. parent/child; brother/sister); or
- the parties have knowingly and wilfully married in breach of the formality requirements.

Apart from this the law is relatively liberal about who can marry. In particular the courts will not prevent a couple marrying because they are marrying for "bad" reasons (e.g. for tax purposes).

KEY CASE ANALYSIS: *R (On the Application to the Crown Prosecution Service) v Registrar General* [2003] EWCA 1222

Background

- A woman was the chief prosecution witness in the case of a man charged with murder.
- The woman and man decided to marry. This would mean under the law of evidence she, as his wife, could not be required to give evidence against him.
- The Crown Prosecution Service sought an injunction to prevent the couple marrying arguing it was against public policy.

Principle established

- It was held there was no power to stop people marrying based on public policy.
- As long as the marriage was not void the couple had a right to marry for whatever reasons they had.

On-the-spot question

? Do you think the law should police the reasons people marry? If so, what would be an unacceptable reason for marrying? One major issue concerns those who marry for immigration purposes. In short, the law accepts they are married, but then does not accept the marriage as sufficient for immigration purposes if there is not a genuine marriage. Is that an appropriate response?

The grounds on which a marriage is void are relatively uncontroversial. Few people would argue that those under 16 should be permitted to marry. Those between 16 and 18 need the consent of a parent with parental responsibility before they can marry. The current law is in line with the age of consent to sex, set at 16. It is generally agreed that under the age of 16 a child lacks the maturity and experience of the world necessary to be able to consent to marriage.

The degrees of prohibited relationship are likewise relatively uncontroversial, but less straightforward to justify than might be thought.

KEY CASE ANALYSIS: *B and L v UK* [2006] 1 FLR 35

Background

- A woman wanted to marry her father in law (her ex-husband's father).
- Under the English law at that time they could not marry as they were within the prohibited degree of relations, although a private members bill before the House of Lords, had in the past allowed marriages between a woman and her father in law.

Principle established

- The European Court of Human Rights (ECtHR) found the bar on marriages between father in law and daughter in law unjustified. The main claim was that a child of a woman would find it confusing if his mother was to marry his grandfather.
- The court replied that if the relationship was taking place, the child would feel confusion, regardless of whether they married or not.
- It was not right for there to be a law generally prohibiting these marriages but then allow exceptions for those rich enough, or well-enough connected, to get a private members bill passed.
- As a result of the decision the prohibition on people marrying their spouses in law was lifted.

FIERCE DEBATE

What exactly is wrong with a brother marrying a sister? Some people rely on the argument that any children of a brother and sister might carry genetic disorders. It is true that the children of closely related parents have a higher risk of genetic disorders, but with modern assisted reproductive technology it is possible to screen embryos before implantation. So a couple could avoid the risk of a disorder. In any event, the couple may not plan to have children, whether or not they are permitted to marry. An alternative argument is that children should be raised in a family setting without any possibility of approved sexual relations. However, it is not clear that the law on prohibiting marriage between family members is a very effective tool against child abuse. Perhaps it is simply a gut reaction that there is "something wrong" with marriage between close relations even if we cannot explain it. It is noticeable that nearly all countries have restrictions on marriage between brothers and sisters. This might be taken to suggest there is something "unnatural" about them. On the other hand relying on such gut instinct might simply be a justification for prejudice.

The law of marriage does not allow someone to marry if they are already married. In other words **polygamy** is not permitted. Of course, there is nothing to stop someone living with numerous partners; it is only marriage that is restricted to one other person. Justification for this restriction is not straightforward to provide in cases where all the parties are happy with the arrangement. It may be that one person cannot be financially responsible for several spouses, but that does not seem a reason to stop a very rich person from having multiple spouses. There may be concerns that there will be tensions between the spouses or their children, but that can be found in many families. In the end the restriction of marriage to two people may come down to a reflection of what society has traditionally thought to be "normal" and "natural".

On-the-spot question

Do you think that the religious understandings of marriage still have too much sway over the law? If people want to marry each other, is there a good reason for not allowing them to? As we have seen the law prohibiting marriages between people who are closely related; those who wish to have more than two people in their marriage; and, until recently, restrictions on same-sex couples marrying hark back to the orthodox teaching of the church. To some, in a secular society, religious understandings of marriage have no role. To others, marriage is in its essence a religious concept and the law should respect that.

The consequences of a void marriage

If a couple enter a void marriage, the court can still award financial relief if they think it is appropriate to do so. That may be suitable where one party is entirely innocent in relation to the circumstances in which the marriage is void. For example, a woman marries a man unaware that he is already married to someone else. Even where a party is aware that the marriage is invalid the court may be persuaded to make an order if there is a particularly strong reason to do so (e.g. one party is in severe financial need).

NON-MARRIAGE

The fact financial consequences can result from a void marriage means it is necessary to distinguish a void marriage from a non-marriage.

Key definition: non-marriage

A non-marriage is a ceremony that is so far from what an effective marriage is like. It is "nothing like a marriage". An example might be a marriage ceremony portrayed in a play; or a group of friends pretending to get married for a laugh.

Where there is a **non-marriage**, this is a "legal nothing" and no legal consequences can flow from it. In particular no financial orders can be made, whatever the needs of the parties.

KEY CASE ANALYSIS: *Hudson v Leigh* [2009] 1 FLR 1129

Background

- The couple went through a ceremony in South Africa, which they realised did not comply with the formality requirements in that country.
- They intended to have a proper formal civil marriage in England. They exchanged rings, but there were no formal documents and no signing of the marriage register.
- When the couple arrived in England they fell out and the issue arose whether the South African ceremony was a void marriage or a non-marriage.

Principle established

The following factors were listed by Body J as relevant in an assessment of whether the marriage was valid:

1. Did the ceremony purport to be a lawful marriage?
2. Did the ceremony bear the hallmarks of the marriage?
3. Did the couple and the official believe, intend and understand the ceremony as creating a lawful marriage?
4. What were the reasonable perceptions, understandings and beliefs of those attending the ceremony?

Applying these to the case Bodey J held that as the couple and the minister who had performed the ceremony realised it was not a legally effective marriage it would be held to be a non-marriage.

THE PRESUMPTION IN FAVOUR OF MARRIAGE

Where a couple have lived together for a considerable period of time and where they are regarded by those who know them to be married then there is a common law presumption that the couple are married. This is rebuttable if there is evidence they were married. This is not normally an issue with marriages within the UK because the register of marriages records all marriages. There is rarely, therefore, an issue about whether a marriage took place or not. However, it can be used in cases where a couple have married overseas.

KEY CASE ANALYSIS: *Pazpena de Vire v Pazpena de Vire* **[2001] 1 FLR 460**

Background

- The couple had married in Uruguay.
- They had come to England and lived as a married couple for 35 years.
- When the wife sought a divorce the husband claimed they had never married.

Principle established

- It was held that they had lived together for such a long time and were regarded by those who knew them as married that this created a strong presumption in favour of marriage.
- The wife did not need to prove that they had married.

SAME-SEX MARRIAGE

It used to be that couples had to belong to the opposite sex to be married. However, that rule was removed by the Marriage (Same-Sex Couples) Act 2013. In a refreshingly clear statement the Act states in section 1: "marriage of same sex couples is lawful".

Unfortunately the position is not quite as clear as this section suggests because there are some differences between same-sex and opposite-sex marriages. Two are particularly notable:

1   The consummation grounds for voidability (see below) apply to opposite-sex marriages, but not same-sex marriages.
2   The adultery fact used to support a divorce petition only covers sex between opposite-sex couples.

This means that although for most practical purposes it no longer matters whether a couple is same sex or opposite sex, it does in a few cases. This means we still need to provide a legal definition of sex.

Key definition: sex

Whether a person is male or female is determined in the law at a person's birth. The assessment is based on their genital, gonadal and chromosomal factors. Psychological factors are not relevant. If a child is born intersex and the genital, gonadal and chromosomal factors are not congruent then other factors including psychological factors can be taken into account. Under the Gender Recognition Act 2004, a person can apply for a Gender Recognition Certificate, which acknowledges they are no longer living in the sex they were registered. This is used by transpeople seeking to have their gender recognised for legal and other purposes.

FIERCE DEBATE

Given the debates over same-sex marriage, would it have been sensible to leave marriage as a religious marriage and create a new legal institution (called, say, civil union) that would be open to all couples? This could have produced legal equality, without creating offence to conservative religious people.

NULLITY

An application to have a marriage annulled may claim that the marriage is void or that it is voidable. A voidable marriage is somewhat different from a void marriage. There are three key differences:

1   A voidable marriage only comes to an end when a court order is made. If there is no court order the voidable marriage will remain valid. A void marriage is always invalid. There is no need for a court order to make it invalid, although a court order may confirm that the marriage is void.
2   A child born to a void marriage is "illegitimate" unless the couple believed their marriage to be valid. A child born to a voidable marriage is not "illegitimate". This distinction is of little practical importance because the law nowadays only very rarely pays attention to whether a child is "illegitimate".
3   Any interested person can apply to have a court confirm a marriage is void. Only the parties to the marriage can have a voidable marriage declared invalid.

The last point is interesting because it highlights an important issue. The grounds on which a marriage is voidable are really only of importance to the couples themselves. The grounds on which a marriage is void indicate a public reason for why the marriage is annulled.

The following are the grounds on which a marriage may be voidable:

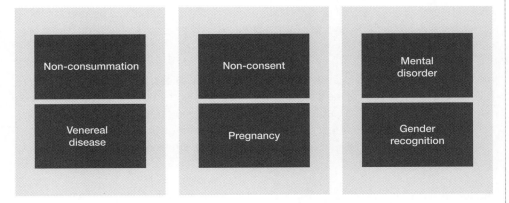

Figure 2.1 Grounds on which a marriage may be voidable

We can say a little more about each.

1 **Non-consummation**. If the marriage has not been consummated due to the incapacity of either party, or due to the wilful refusal of the other party. You cannot rely on your own wilful refusal to consummate in order to have the marriage annulled.
2 **Non-consent**. Either party to the marriage did not consent to the marriage. That may be as a result of duress, mistake or unsoundness of mind. Notably here you can rely on the other party's lack of consent to the marriage as the basis of an annulment. It is also worth emphasising that this ground only renders a marriage voidable. So if one person was forced to marry another person, but in fact they got on well, the marriage could continue as a valid marriage.
3 **Mental disorder**. Either party suffered a mental disorder and so was unfit for marriage. This must be a mental disorder that existed when the couple married. If a mental disorder developed after the marriage then divorce proceedings would need to be issued if the spouse wanted to end the marriage.
4 **Venereal disease**. The other party suffered from communicable venereal disease.
5 **Pregnancy**. At the time of the marriage the other party was pregnant by someone other than the husband.
6 **Gender Recognition Certificate**. The other party had a Gender Recognition Certificate, but the applicant was not aware of this.

We can say a little more about some of these.

Lack of consent

Lack of consent to the marriage can arise from several causes. Mistake is included, but this will only apply where there is a fundamental mistake, such as a mistake about the identity of the person you are marrying. A mistake about the attributes of a spouse, such as their wealth or age, will not be sufficient. However, a belief that the person you are marrying is X, when in fact they are Y, would be sufficient to negate consent. Similarly, a belief that the ceremony is not a marriage ceremony but a birthday party or engagement party would be sufficient.

Most cases of lack of consent have involved allegations of duress. Following *Hirani v Hirani* [1982] the court will focus of the impact on the threat, rather than the kind of threat. So it is not necessary to show there was a threat of death or serious violence. However, it is necessary to show that the threat had such an impact on the victim that she did not consent to marriage. This includes cases where there was emotional or family pressure, as well as physical threats.

Quite a few cases in recent years have involved forced marriages and the Forced Marriage (Civil Protection) Act 2007 deals with this. It is important to distinguish a forced marriage, where a party's choice is severely constrained and an arranged marriage where the parents might encourage a child to marry a person of their choice, but there is no improper pressure involved.

KEY CASE ANALYSIS: *B v I (Forced Marriage)* [2010] 1 FLR 1721

Background

- A 16-year-old girl travelled to Bangladesh from England.
- She thought she was being taken on a holiday but she was married to her 18-year-old cousin.
- On her return to England she successfully sought the inherent jurisdiction to declare the marriage was void.

Principle established

- Considerable psychological and emotional pressure had been put on her to marry and she was in an unfamiliar country with no friends to support her.
- The marriage should, therefore, be regarded as void.

Under the Forced Marriage (Civil Protection) Act 2007, if the court is concerned that a forced marriage is to take place it can make a range of orders designed to prevent the marriage occurring. These can include an order that someone's passport be given up to the court.

Non-consummation

As already mentioned, the non-consummation grounds only apply to opposite-sex couples. Many commentators view this as an outdated requirement. If a couple have not had sex does that really invalidate the marriage? This requirement seems a hangover from the ecclesiastical church regulation of marriage when consummation had a theological role to play in the nature of marriage. It does not seem to have a good ongoing justification. This is especially as a single act of sexual intercourse is sufficient to consummate a marriage. This means it cannot really be used as a means of ensuring the marriage was a happy one.

Capacity

An issue that has troubled the courts on several occasions is whether someone has the capacity to marry. Typically the case involves a person with severe learning difficulties who is seeking to marry. There is general agreement that there can be no objection to those with mild learning disabilities marrying, but what about those whose understanding is more severely impaired? The issues are even harder when there is a suspicion that the person they wish to marry is in danger of exploiting them.

KEY CASE ANALYSIS: *Sheffield CC v E* [2005] Fam 326

Background

- A young woman was 21 years old, but said to function as a 13-year-old. She had a number of learning difficulties.
- She befriended an older man who had a history of sexually violent crimes. They planned to marry.
- The local authority sought an order to prevent the marriage.

Principle established

- Munby J confirmed that it was presumed a person had capacity to marry. Those seeking to suggest otherwise had to persuade the court that the person lacked capacity.

- To have capacity to marry it was only necessary to understand the nature of marriage and the duties and responsibilities of marriage. These were that the couple would live together, love one another to the exclusion of others, share a common home and domestic life, and enjoy each other's society, comfort and assistance.
- Munby J did not think that a high degree of intelligence was required to understand these. He thought it would be wrong if the courts considered the suitability of a person's partner.
- The focus must be on their capacity to marry not whether they were wise to marry the person they chose.

FIERCE DEBATE

Should those with significant learning disabilities be permitted to marry? If a couple are in love does it matter that they may have intellectual impairments? Does your attitude change if one party to the marriage has a significant intellectual impairment but the other does not?

Bars to nullity

Even if an applicant can show one of the voidable grounds section 13 of the Matrimonial Causes Act lists four bars that can prevent a marriage being annulled:

1   Approbation. This deals with cases where the petitioner knew that they could have had the marriage annulled but behaved in such a way that the respondent believed they would not. For example, imagine during the honeymoon a man discovers that his bride is pregnant by another man, but tells her this does not bother him. He could not later seek to annul the marriage on that basis.

2   Three-year bar. If the applicant is relying on any of the bars, except those based on consummation, they must apply within three years of the marriage. This seems to be a form of assumed approbation. If the application has not challenged the marriage within three years it can be taken that the spouse was willing to continue the marriage despite the difficulties. Consummation is excluded presumably on the basis that some couples may require more than three years to attempt consummation.

3   If the issuing of a Gender Recognition Certificate is relied upon then the proceeding must be issued within six months of the marriage.

4   The pregnancy, venereal disease and Gender Recognition Certificate grounds cannot be relied upon unless the court is satisfied that the petitioner was ignorant of the facts at the time of the marriage.

CIVIL PARTNERSHIP

Civil partnerships were created by the 2004 Civil Partnership Act. They are only open to couples of the same sex. They were originally created to enable same-sex couples to have the same legal rights as married couples. Now same-sex couples can marry, it is possible the status will fall into disuse, although it may appeal to those same-sex couples who feel that the word "marriage" has religious connotations they would rather avoid. In 2014 the Government announced there were no plans to extend civil partnership to opposite-sex couples. However, same-sex couples in a civil partnership could convert their civil partnerships into a marriage from November 2014, if they wished.

Like marriage, civil partnership is not open to those who already have civil partners or are married; those under 16; or those within the prohibited degrees of relationship. The legal regulation of civil partnership and marriage are very similar. Indeed one judge described civil partnership as "marriage in all but name". There are some differences between civil partnership and opposite-sex marriage and they are similar to the differences between same and opposite-sex partnership: Adultery cannot be used as a fact for divorce; non-consummation cannot be a ground for rendering a marriage voidable; and venereal disease cannot render a civil partnership voidable.

> **On-the-spot question**
>
> Should civil partnership be open to opposite-sex as well as same-sex couples? The argument in favour of doing so is that civil partnership offers an alternative to marriage, with its religious overtones, to those who wish to avoid the traditional trappings of marriage. Should that not be open to opposite-sex couples as well as same-sex couples? Or should we abolish civil partnership altogether and just have marriage? Or indeed abolish marriage and just have civil partnership?

DISTINGUISHING MARRIAGE AND COHABITATION

Does it matter whether you are married or are in a civil partnership (CP)? It can do in the following situations:

1   The end of the relationship. Marriage and CP can only be ended by an order of the court. Cohabitation can be ended by the parties simply deciding to live apart.

2   Redistribution of property. At the end of a marriage or CP the court has extensive power to make financial orders. At the end of a cohabitation the court has no power to redistribute property.

3   Financial support. During a marriage, one spouse can seek financial support from the other (Domestic Proceedings and Magistrates Court Act 1978). Cohabitants owe each other no duty of financial support. Of course, child support can be ordered whether the couple are married or not, but that is designed to meet the needs of the child not the parent caring for the child.

4   Parental responsibility. A married father automatically gets parental responsibility. An unmarried father needs to be registered on the child's birth certificate; enter a parental responsibility agreement with the mother; or apply to the court for a parental responsibility order.

5   Intestacy. If a spouse dies with no will, their spouse will acquire all or most of their property. If a person dies with a cohabitant they will acquire nothing automatically and must seek a court order to do so.

6   Tax. A married couple can claim tax exemption in relation to inheritance tax and capital gains tax. Cohabitants do not acquire these.

MARRIAGE AS A STATUS

One of the important things to remember about marriage is that it is a status. This was emphasised by Baroness Hale in *Radmacher v Granatino* [2010]. She called marriage a status in the sense that the marriage is a "package which the law of the land lays down". So you cannot enter marriage and then say, "I want to marry but I don't want to be liable to pay financial support to my spouse". You must either take the package of marriage as offered by the law or leave it. That approach is somewhat under challenge: as we shall see in Chapter 4 in *Radmacher v Granatino* the Supreme Court accepted that the parties can enter into a pre-marriage agreement and so set out the terms of the marriage. However, the courts will not enforce these if that would be unfair. In essence, although there are some aspects of marriage the couple can choose for themselves, the basic foundations of marriage cannot be changed.

SUMMARY

*   Marriages can be entered into by unmarried couples who are over the age of 16 and not too closely related.

- A marriage can be voidable on various grounds including non-consummation, pregnancy and venereal disease.
- While there are some important differences between being married and not, in many areas of law there is no difference.

FURTHER READING

R Auchmuty, "What's so special about marriage? The impact of *Wilkinson v Kitzinger*" (2008) 20 *Child and Family Law Quarterly* 475 – considers whether marriage is significant today.

N Barker, *Not the Marrying Kind: A Feminist Critique of Same-Sex Marriage* (Macmillan, 2012) – argues against same-sex marriage from a feminist perspective.

E Brake, *Minimising Marriage* (Oxford University Press, 2012) – argues for a reduced significance for marriage.

P-L Chau and J Herring, "Men, women and people: The definition of sex" in B Brooks-Gordon, L Goldsthorpe, M Johnson and A Bainham (eds) *Sexuality Repositioned* (Hart, 2004) – discusses the definition of sex for the purposes of marriage.

R Deech, "Cohabitation" (2010) 40 *Family Law* 39 – discusses the phenomenon of cohabitation.

R Gaffney Rhys, "The concept of the forced marriage" (2010) *Child and Family Law Quarterly* 351 – considers the nature of forced marriage.

S Girgis, R George and T Anderson, "What is marriage?" (2010) *Harvard Journal of Law and Public Policy* 245 – argues against permitting same-sex marriage.

L Green, "Sex-neutral marriage" (2011) 64 *Current Legal Problems* 1 – examines the role of sex within marriage.

G Pearce and A Gill, "Criminalising forced marriage through stand-alone legalisation: Will it work?" (2012) *Family Law* 534 – considers whether forced marriage should be a criminal offence.

Chapter 3
Informal families

After reading this chapter you should be able to:

- understand the legal regulation of property disputes between unmarried couples;
- explain the concept of a constructive trust;
- understand the meaning of proprietary estoppel;
- explore potential reforms of the law on unmarried couples.

INTRODUCTION

It used to be assumed that couples who wanted to set up a family would get married. Although marriage is still a popular option many people prefer to find informal family arrangements. This can range from a couple living together matching in many ways the traditional appearance of marriage, but without going through the paperwork; to people "living apart together", who regard themselves as being in a committed relationship but do not live in the same home; to "friends with benefits" who have a sexual relationship but with a minimal sense of commitment.

These informal relationships are difficult for the law to deal with, partly because they cover such a range of cases. It is difficult to know the extent to which the couple have undertaken commitments or obligations to each other. In many cases it may well be that one party regards the relationship as far more serious than the other, in which case whose understanding should the law adopt? Indeed it may not be especially helpful to use the term "cohabitants" because that term covers so many different kinds of relationships.

The traditional approach is that those who are not married are treated in the same way as strangers. If they choose to avoid marriage and not have their relationship formally recognised the law should respect that. However, that view is increasingly under challenge. Many couples do not realise if they fail to marry they have few legal rights. It seems that many believe the so-called "common-law marriage myth", which says that couples who live together are treated by the law as married. That is a false, but persistent, belief. Others never really consider the legal ramifications of their intimate lives. So although the starting point is that they are legally strangers, there is a range of statutory provisions that now cover informal relationships.

REAL WORLD

In 2001 12.5 per cent of all families involved a cohabiting couple. By 2011 this had risen to 16 per cent. Add to this the 16 per cent of families that are lone parents and you can see the extent of cohabitation. Perhaps most notably 47 per cent of births are recorded by mothers who are not married. That figure has steadily risen and it will soon be the case that the odds are that a child will be born outside marriage. The vast majority of married couples live together before marrying.

STATUTORY RECOGNITION

There are a host of statutes that give the same rights to unmarried couples as to married couples. However, typically this is restricted to couples who are living together in the same way as a married couple. This might cause some problems for those in a relationship that does not match a conventional marriage, such as those who are "living apart together". A good example of statutory recognition is the Rent Act 1977, which gives unmarried couples living together "as husband and wife" exactly the same rights as couples.

KEY CASE ANALYSIS: *Ghaidan v Godin-Mondoza* [2004] 2 AC 556

Background

- Mr Wallwyn-James was the tenant of a flat he lived in with his partner Mr Godin-Mendoza.
- Mr Wallwyn-James died. This would have brought the tenancy to an end, unless Mr Godin-Mendoza was entitled to claim the tenancy under the terms of the Rent Act 1977. He sought to do so claiming he was living as "husband and wife" with the tenant.

Principle established

- The House of Lords interpreted the phrase "living together as husband and wife" to include a same-sex couple in a committed relationship. They relied

on the Human Rights Act 1998 to achieve this result, explaining that the interpretation ensured there was no discrimination against same-sex couples.
- Their lordships also believed the public policy behind allowing opposite-sex couples to use the Act applied equally well to same-sex couples.

PROPERTY DISPUTES ON SEPARATION

We will look at the position of married couples and their property in Chapter 5. The court on divorce has the power to order one party to pay the other monthly payments or transfer to their spouse sums of money or even property. It is very different for those who are not married. The court has no power to order one cohabitant to pay money to the other. So while the spouse of a multi-millionaire might expect at the end of the relationship to receive a reasonable proportion of the wealth, perhaps even half, the **cohabitant** of a millionaire can expect none of his property. All the court can do in the case of cohabitants is declare who owns what. It cannot change ownership.

As an aside, it is different in relation to children. Children are entitled to child support whether their parents are married or not. So the child of the millionaire can expect financial support during their childhood whether their parents are married or not. Indeed the courts have suggested that the children of millionaires should live an appropriate kind of lifestyle, whether their parents are married or not. This might include the child living in a luxurious house and, of course, the parent with care of the child would benefit from that.

PERSONAL PROPERTY

The basic law on personal property is that the person who buys the item is the owner, but that ownership of the item can be transferred by a gift or creation of a **trust**. There are no

Key definition: personal property

Personal property is property apart from land. It would include household items such as televisions or computers, and also money and investments. Land is known as real property and is not included in the definition of personal property.

formal requirements over these and casual comments in conversation can be said to create a trust. Similarly the court may infer a gift from the facts of the case. If the husband buys some jewellery and gives it to his wife, it will, no doubt, be presumed that he intended to pass ownership of it to her. That is always subject to the particular facts of the case. So if a husband gave his wife some jewellery adding that it had been in his family for generations, but she could borrow it, this would make it clear that a gift was not intended.

KEY CASE ANALYSIS: *Rowe v Prance* [1999] 2 FLR 787

Background

- A man owned a valuable yacht.
- He had been in a lengthy relationship with the claimant. She had not contributed financially to the purchase of the yacht.
- There was evidence that the man had spoken of "our boat" and of "a share of the boat together".

Principle established

It was held that these words were sufficient to indicate that the boat was held on trust and the claimant was entitled to a share in the boat. There was no need to use formal language of a trust, but talk of sharing was sufficient.

LAND

Most property disputes involve land. Land is now registered at the Land Registry and a straightforward search can determine who is the registered owner. This will tell you who is the owner at common law, but that is not the end of the case. The registered owner may hold the property on trust. So if the cohabitant is not one of the registered owners and wants to make a claim they will need to argue there is an express trust, a constructive trust, or a proprietary estoppel.

Express trust of land

An express trust of land can only be created by writing (s 53, Law of Property Act 1925). So in the absence of formal documentation the cohabitant will need to rely on one of the other forms of a trust.

Key definition: trust

In a trust one person owns a piece of property in common law. They are the trustees. They hold the property on behalf of the beneficiaries who own the property in equity. A common form of trust is where an adult holds property on trust on behalf of a child. Ultimately it is the beneficiaries who control what happens to the property and can require the sale of the trust property and that they be paid their share of the proceeds. It is possible for a person to be both a trustee and a beneficiary.

Key definition: resulting trust

A resulting trust arises where one person (A) contributes to the purchase price of a piece of property, which is put into the name of another (B). In such a case, unless there is clear evidence that this was not the intention of the parties, B will hold the property on trust for A and whoever else contributed to the party. That is the presumption. It can be rebutted by clear evidence to the contrary. You can imagine a case where a parent buys a property and puts it into her daughter's name, not intending the daughter to hold the property on trust.

If A contributed all the purchase price for a property put into B's name, B would hold on trust for A absolutely. However, if A and B contributed equally B would hold on trust for A and B in equal shares. This is a rebuttable presumption, so if there was clear evidence that A intended the property to be a gift for B (perhaps she was his relative) the presumption of a trust would not arise and B would hold the property absolutely.

The courts have held that in the areas of disputes between unmarried couples, resulting trusts have relatively little role to play. That is because, as we shall see, if one person contributes to the purchase price this will give rise to a constructive trust and they are likely to get a larger share under that kind of trust than they would under a resulting trust. So anyone who could claim a resulting trust might as well claim a constructive trust.

CONSTRUCTIVE TRUSTS

Key definition: constructive trusts

Two things must be shown to establish a constructive trust:

1   There is a common intention to share ownership. There must be an express agreement to share ownership or the agreement can be inferred from, for example, a contribution to the purchase price.
2   Actions by the claimant in reliance on the common intention.

KEY CASE ANALYSIS: *Lloyds Bank v Rosset* [1990] 2 FLR 155

Background

- The case concerned a married couple.
- The house was purchased in the husband's name.
- Mrs Rosset had helped renovate the property but had not contributed financially to its purchase or renovation.
- Mr Rosset took out a mortgage on the property but failed to make the required payments.
- When the bank sought possession of the house Mrs Rosset claimed she had a share in the property under a constructive trust.

Principle established

- It was held to claim a constructive trust it had to be shown that there was an agreement to share ownership and that she had relied to her detriment on the agreement.
- In this case there was no express agreement to share. Although the House of Lords said they would be willing to infer an agreement to share from a direct contribution to the purchase price or to a mortgage instalment, Mrs Rosset had made neither of these. She could not, therefore, claim a share in the property.

The first element of a constructive trust requires proof of a common intention to share ownership. This will normally be proved by evidence of a conversation between the two parties. There is no need to show a formal discussion. Talk of "our house" may be enough. In *Eves v Eves* [1975] the man saying (untruthfully) the woman was too young to be put on the deeds of their house was found to be an implied agreement that they shared the property. That is because he was impliedly telling her that though the house was jointly owned there was a bureaucratic requirement which prevented that being officially recorded. That case suggests the courts will focus on what the parties represent to the other is their intention, rather than what their actual intention was. In *Eves v Eves* [1975] his actual intention seems to have been to deprive her of an interest in the property. But he led her to believe he agreed she had a share in the property.

If there is no conversation that can be relied upon, then the court can find an intention to share to be implied by the way they organised their finances. So, for example, if the claimant contributed to the purchase price, or to a mortgage instalment, this will be seen as evidence of an intention to share. Why otherwise would someone pay such money, or the owner accept it? Some recent cases (e.g. *Abbott v Abbott* [2007]) have suggested that the courts can infer an agreement to share ownership from the more general way the couple arranged their finances. So if the woman paid all the other bills so that the husband could pay the mortgage this might be seen as in effect her contributing to the mortgage payments, in that the man could not have paid them but for her payment of other household bills. It might even be that the court will be willing to find an agreement to share based on the general way they lived together. Were they living a communal kind of life? However, there is no clear authority supporting that approach yet. Generally the courts have been rather wary about doing this unless there is convincing evidence of the parties' intention.

It is worth emphasising that it must be shown that the parties agreed to share ownership. This is not the same thing as agreeing to share possession. So, if a girlfriend says to her boyfriend "come and live with me in my house", that on its own indicates an intention to share possession, but not ownership.

FIERCE DEBATE

The courts have been wary about inferring an agreement to share in the absence of an express conversation. On the one hand there is a danger that the owner of a property who invites someone in on a casual basis will be found to have agreed to share ownership. On the other, in many relationships there is no express agreement about sharing and everything is left unspoken. Do you think the courts should be more willing to infer ownership from the general nature of the relationship? Or should they stick to the approach of requiring a contribution to the financial upkeep of the house?

The second requirement is that the claimant relied on the promise to their detriment. This is generally unproblematic. If the claimant has spent money on the house or has put themselves in a vulnerable position by moving into the house they will be able to show that they have relied on the promise.

KEY CASE ANALYSIS: *Thomson v Humphrey* [2009] EWHC 3576 (Ch)

Background

- A man lived in a property that was in his name.
- The female cohabitant moved in with him with her children, giving up her part-time job. He had said he would look after her.

Principle established

- It was held the promise to "look after her" was not sufficient to create an agreement to share.
- Even if it was true that she had given up a poorly paid job, there was not sufficient detrimental reliance on any promise to constitute a share.

Having ascertained a constructive trust has been created the court must decide what share each party has. The short answer is that the share will be what both parties agree. The difficulty arises where that is not clear. In such a case the court must do its best to determine what their intentions were by looking at all the surrounding evidence.

KEY CASE ANALYSIS: *Jones v Kernott* [2011] UKSC 53

Background

- Mr Kernott and Ms Jones bought a house in joint names. They had two children together.
- Ms Jones paid all the outgoings and the mortgage.
- After the relationship ended Mr Kernott moved out and Ms Jones lived there, paying the expense for a further 15 years.

Principle

- The property was in joint names. Generally it would be presumed that the couple intended to hold the property equally on trust in 50/50 shares. However, that presumption could be rebutted if there is evidence to the contrary.
- Normally a court would use evidence of their actual agreement, but if there was none, then inferences could be drawn from their conduct and their relationship.
- Given the length of time Ms Jones lived alone in the property and her much more significant financial contribution it was inferred that she was to have a 90 per cent share in the property and Mr Kernott a 10 per cent share.

On-the-spot question

 If a couple have put a property in joint names should we not conclusively presume they intend the property to be jointly owned in equity as well as law? Are there dangers in reading too much into "who paid for what" in a relationship?

PROPRIETARY ESTOPPEL

Key definition: proprietary estoppel

If A wishes to claim a proprietary estoppel over B's property the points shown in Figure 3.1 must be established:

A promised B an
interest in the property

B relied on the promise
to their detriment

It would be conscionable to give
A an interest in the property

Figure 3.1 Elements of a proprietary estoppel

The law on proprietary estoppel tends to be generally strict on requiring a clear promise over a property. There must be more than a promise that someone can live in a house; it must be a promise that they will have a share in the ownership of the house. Similarly a vague promise along the lines of "I will look after you" will be insufficient as it does not clearly indicate it is the house that is being promised. It may be that a propriety estoppel can be based on a somewhat vague promise if there is substantial reliance on it (*Wayling v Jones* [1995]). So if A makes a vague promise about B having a share in the property and then stands by as B relies on the vague assurance significantly to B's detriment it may be sufficient to establish a propriety estoppel. Even then the courts will require that the vague promise related to the property. Perhaps a promise along the lines "you will never need to leave this property" would be sufficient if there was significant detrimental reliance. Conversely, if there is a very clear promise then less detriment may be required. Notably in *Gillett v Holt* [2000] the Court of Appeal emphasised that the concept of **unconscionability** was at the heart of propriety estoppel. They emphasised it was less a matter of having strict rules and more a matter of seeking to find out what would be fair in the circumstances of the case.

KEY CASE ANALYSIS: *Thorner v Major* [2009] UKHL 18

Background

- Mr Thorner had worked for his cousin on a farm for 29 years. He never received any pay. The cousin was "a man of few words".
- Thorner admitted there was little discussion about ownership of the farm, but believed there was an unspoken agreement he would be left the farm.
- Indeed the cousin gave Thorner a life insurance policy "to pay for death duties". This reinforced Thorner's belief that the cousin would leave him the farm.
- In fact on his death the cousin left the farm to his siblings.

Principle established

- For a propriety estoppel the promise had to be clear enough. The key question would be whether it was reasonable for the claimant to take the words or conduct as an assurance on which it is reasonable to rely.
- In a case like this with a man of few words, it would not be reasonable to expect a clear assurance. Nevertheless, ultimately the claim failed.
- Although Thorner had reason to believe he would be left something in the will, there was not a clear promise it would be the farm. And propriety estoppel can only relate to promises in relation to identified property.

REFORM

Many people believe that the law on property orders and cohabitants needs reform. Famously in *Burns v Burns* [1984], at the end of a very lengthy unmarried relationship (the woman took the man's name, but they never married) the woman was left with nothing because she could not identify a clear statement from her partner that she had a share in the house. This seems unfair to many people.

Some jurisdictions, such as New South Wales in Australia have a rule that if a couple have lived together for a certain period of years (for example, two years) or they have children, then they can be treated as a married couple. Others object to this proposal on the basis that it is wrong that people end up being treated as married when they have not specifically agreed to take on the obligations of marriage. However, jurisdictions that have this kind of provision allow for a couple to opt out of the arrangement if they wish. Still some feel that serious financial obligations should be something you choose rather than need to opt out of.

The Law Commission produced a detailed report on the issue in 2007. Their proposals, in brief, are that the courts should be given the power to redistribute the property of couples who have cohabited but only to the extent that is necessary to ensure a party is compensated for an economic sacrifice during the relationship or if one party has made an economic gain from the relationship. This is less extensive than for married couples, but provides more scope for intervention than the current law does.

FIERCE DEBATE

Many of the proposals for reform indicate there should be an opt out possibility. This is not uncontroversial. Let us imagine a couple, Anne and Robert, who have lived together for ten years. They have adopted "traditional" roles. Robert has developed his career and now earns a substantial salary. He has amassed an impressive investment portfolio and he has bought a mansion, put into his name. Anne has been fully supportive of his career and enabled him to progress as far as he has. She has organised fabulous dinner parties for his business contacts, which have been used to secure numerous important deals. She has undertaken nearly all the care of their children. At the end of their relationship the current approach could leave Anne with nothing, if she is not able to establish a trust of some kind. Under the Law Commission Reforms and the NSW approach, Anne would be likely to receive significant recognition for her work. But under both, she would not if the couple opted out of the scheme.

On the one hand, this is seen as unproblematic. If the couple choose to live their life outside the scheme, then that is their choice. People are free to give their money to others as gifts, however unwise other people may think that is. It is all a matter of freedom. However, others disagree and argue one cannot opt out of a matter of justice. The minimum wage legislation, for example, prohibits an employer paying the employee a very low sum of money, even if the employee approves of it. Similarly, an employer cannot pay people of different races different rates for the same work, even if the workforce does not object. These demonstrate that there are certain principles of justice you cannot opt out of. However, not everyone will agree that financial orders at the end of a relationship fall within this category.

PROPERTY ON DEATH

When a person dies the law is fairly straightforward if they have left a will. The property will be distributed in accordance with the will. If the person has not left a will then their estate is "intestate" and there is a statutory scheme that governs how the property is left. This is complex, but in essence that statute predicts where the deceased would have wanted their assets to go. If the deceased is married then all or most of their estate will go to their spouse. If they are not married it will go to their children, or other close relatives. A cohabitant is not mentioned in the intestacy rules. So if someone is cohabiting and dies without leaving a will, under the automatic rules the cohabitant will get nothing.

All is not lost, however, for the cohabitant because if a person's will or the rules on **intestacy** produce a result someone thinks is unfair then they can challenge the allocation by applying under the Inheritance (Provision for Families and Dependants) Act 1975. The application is likely to succeed if brought by a spouse. The courts will not allow, say, a husband to leave his wife nothing in his will. If a husband attempts to do this the court is likely to award the wife a sum similar to what she would have received had she divorced him. She may even get more than that because there is no need for his needs to be considered when deciding what is a fair distribution.

A cohabitant can claim under the 1975 Act. A cohabitant is defined in s 1 (1A) and (1B) as:

> a person who was living in the same household as the deceased during the whole of two years ending immediately before the date of the deceased's death and was living as the husband or wife or civil partner of the deceased.

Note this does not apply to a former partner.

> ## KEY CASE ANALYSIS: *Re Watson* [1999] 1 FLR 878
>
> ### Background
>
> A couple in their fifties moved in together. They did not have a sexual relationship but otherwise lived a life together.
>
> ### Principle established
>
> Held that the test to apply was whether "in the opinion of a reasonable person with ordinary perceptions, it could be said that the two people in question were living together as husband and wife". This did not require a sexual relationship, although it required a sharing of lives.

If a cohabitant claims, they will only be permitted to seek an award for maintenance. That means their basic needs will be met, but they will not be entitled to share in the wealth of their partner based simply on the fact they lived together.

Former cohabitants will need to claim they were being maintained by the deceased (s 1(1)(e)). This requires proof that they were receiving financial support from the deceased, which met their needs. So, more than being gifts would be required.

SUMMARY

- Generally informal relationships are recognised by the law, although they can be in statute.
- If an informal relationship comes to an end the court cannot redistribute property, but it can declare who owns what.
- If there is an agreement to share ownership of a house the court may find that a constructive trust has been created.
- If the owners of a house make a promise that another person will have a share in it this can create a proprietary estoppel.

FURTHER READING

G Battersby, "Ownership of the family law: *Stack v Dowden* in the House of Lords" (2008) *Child and Family Law Quarterly* 255 – examines the case of Stack v Dowden.

M Dixon, "Confining and defining proprietary estoppel: The role of unconscionability" (2010) 30 *Legal Studies* 408 – considers the law on proprietary estoppel.

S Gardner, "Family property today" (2008) 112 *Law Quarterly Review* 263 – provides an overview of the law on constructive trusts.

S Gardner and K Davidson, "The future of *Stack v Dowden*" (2011) 127 *Law Quarterly Review* 13 – considers the impact of *Stack v Dowden*.

S Hayward, "'Family property' and the process of 'familisiation of property law'" (2012) *Child and Family Law Quarterly* 284 – looks at the interaction of family law and property law.

Chapter 4
Divorce

LEARNING OBJECTIVES

After reading this chapter you should be able to:

- explain the ground for divorce;
- state the facts that can prove the ground for divorce;
- discuss possible reforms to the law on divorce;
- describe the differences between divorce and dissolution.

INTRODUCTION

It is said that **divorce** is one of the most stressful experiences a person can face. There is widespread agreement that the law does little to limit the bitterness and acrimony that so often accompanies it. In this chapter we will look at what must be shown if a marriage is to be ended by divorce or a civil partnership by dissolution. We will also consider how the law may be reformed given some of the concerns with it.

This chapter will consider the law on divorce and dissolution of a civil partnership. Fortunately the two are very similar. The law on divorce is also one of the few areas of the law where there is a difference between marriages of parties of the same sex and those of the opposite sex. That will be explained in this chapter.

REAL WORLD

There was a five-fold increase in the divorce rate between 1961 and 1991. There were 4.7 divorces per 1,000 marriages in 1970, which rose to 13.7 by 1999. However in 2011 the number had dropped to 11.1. The median length of a marriage is around 11 years.

THE GROUND FOR DIVORCE OR DISSOLUTION

There is only one ground for divorce: that the marriage has broken down irretrievably (Matrimonial Causes Act 1973). The same is true of dissolution of a civil partnership: it must be shown that the civil partnership has broken down irretrievably. However, it is only possible to prove that the marriage or civil partnership has broken down irretrievably if you can prove one of the stated facts exists. Even if you could persuade a judge that the relationship had truly come to an end, if one of the facts is not proved then the judge cannot grant a divorce or dissolution. Similarly if one of the facts is proved but the judge concludes the marriage has not in fact broken down then a divorce will not be granted (s 1(4) Matrimonial Causes Act 1973). That occurs very rarely indeed.

KEY CASE ANALYSIS: *Buffery v Buffery* [1988] 2 FLR 365

Background

- The married couple had nothing in common and they no longer communicated.
- The couple's relationship had broken down.
- None of the facts could be proved.

Principle established

A divorce could not be granted if none of the facts was shown, even if the relationship had broken down.

On-the-spot question

? Why do you think you should need to establish both one of the facts and the fact the marriage has broken down? If a party demonstrates that their marriage has broken down, why should it matter whether it happens to be because of one of the five listed facts?

THE FACTS

Adultery

This fact can only be relied upon in divorce. It does not apply in cases of civil partnership. If a civil partner wishes to rely on sexual misbehaviour they must rely on one of the other grounds.

Key definition: adultery ground

The Matrimonial Causes Act 1973, s 1(2)(1) describes the **adultery** ground as follows: "the respondent has committed adultery and the petitioner finds it intolerable to live with the respondent".

There are two points in particular to notice about the adultery ground. First, the **petitioner** cannot rely on their own adultery to seek a divorce. They can only rely on the adultery of the respondent. Second, it should be noted that it is not enough to show that the **respondent** has committed adultery. It must be shown that the petitioner cannot reasonably be expected to live with him or her. So if the husband forgave the wife after she committed adultery and they were reconciled, but sometime later their relationship broke down and he sought to divorce relying on the wife's adultery, he might fail. He would struggle to show he had found it intolerable to live with his wife.

Key definition: adultery

The Matrimonial Causes Act 1973, s 1(6) defines adultery as: voluntary sexual intercourse between a man and a woman, one of whom is married. Sexual intercourse between people of the same sex is not adultery.

KEY CASE ANALYSIS: *Clearly v Cleary* **[1974] 1 WLR 73**

Background

The wife claimed that the husband had committed adultery and that she found it intolerable to live with him.

Principle established

It was not necessary to show that intolerability was caused by the adultery. It was enough that there was adultery and the petitioner found it intolerable to live with the applicant.

FIERCE DEBATE

There has been much discussion about why adultery should be restricted to opposite sex couples. Notably the Marriage (Same-Sex Couples) Act 2013 made it clear that it only applies to sexual relations between opposite-sex couples. Some commentators have suggested this was because it is hard to define what act would be adultery in same-sex relationships. Others suggest the law is still latently homophobic and unwilling to look same-sex activity "in the face".

REAL WORLD

Although on the divorce petition it is possible to state the third party with whom adultery was committed, practitioners are strongly discouraged from doing this. It is seen as simply increasing antagonism between the parties and creating unnecessary embarrassment. Indeed for these reasons some practitioners avoid using the adultery ground altogether.

Behaviour

Key definition: behaviour

"The respondent has behaved in such a way that the petitioner cannot reasonably be expected to live with the respondent" (Matrimonial Causes Act 1973, section 1).

Notice that the petitioner can only rely on the unreasonable behaviour of the respondent and cannot rely on his or her own behaviour. There would, of course, be something odd about a petitioner seeking a divorce based on the fact that they had behaved badly! Notice that the behaviour must be such that the petitioner cannot reasonably be expected to live with him or her. That indicates that the assessment is to be made based on what is reasonable for a petitioner. So the character and personality of the petitioner is to be considered. A spouse who is obsessive about cleanliness and tidiness may not reasonably be expected to live with a spouse who is dirty and untidy, even though most people would not find that a problem.

The kinds of behaviour that would be likely to feature under this heading could be: violence; verbal abuse; unreasonable demands; or sexual unfaithfulness (including behaviour that would not constitute adultery). However, it seems that there must be some acts and omissions that do not count. A lack of displaying affection was found not to fall under this heading (*Pheasant v Pheasant* [1972]). It is also worth noting that the question is not whether the respondent is to blame for his behaviour. In *Katz v Katz* [1972] a wife was able to divorce her husband who had manic depression, even though his behaviour was not his fault. The focus is more on the impact of the behaviour on the petitioner, rather than whether the respondent has behaved in a reprehensible way.

KEY CASE ANALYSIS: *Livingstone-Stallard v Livingstone-Stallard* [1974] 3 All ER 76

Background

The wife complained about the husband's behaviour, including the way he washed his underwear.

Principle established

The court held the key question was:

> Would any right-thinking person come to the conclusion that this husband has behaved in such a way that his wife cannot reasonably be expected to live with him, taking into account the whole of the circumstances and the characters and personalities of the parties.

KEY CASE ANALYSIS: *Thurlow v Thurlow* [1976] Fam 32

Background

A husband sought to divorce his wife who had become bedridden and lived in a hospital.

Principle established

Even though the party may not be responsible for their behaviour, it can still be relied upon to form the basis for a divorce petition based on behaviour.

On-the-spot question

Do you think it right that an innocent spouse can be divorced against their will? In the *Thurlow* case, for example, it was not the wife's fault she was confined to hospital. You cannot dismiss an employee unless they have behaved wrongly. Should you be able to divorce a blameless spouse?

Desertion

Key definition: desertion

The Matrimonial Causes Act 1973, s 1(2)(c) defines desertion as follows: "The respondent has deserted the petitioner for a continuous period of at least two years immediately preceding the presentation of the petition."

Desertion occurs where there has been actual separation for no good reason and without consent, for two years. It is rarely relied upon.

KEY CASE ANALYSIS: *Le Brocq v Le Brocq* **[1964] 1 WLR 1085**

Background

After fierce disagreements the wife excluded her husband from their bedroom by putting a bolt on the door and he slept in another bedroom. They did not talk; however, the wife did cook for him and he paid her housekeeping money.

Principle established

Desertion requires more than a separation of bedrooms. The couple must no longer operate as a single household.

Two years separation

Key definition: two years separation

The Matrimonial Causes Act 1973 s 1(2)(d) defines two years separation as follows: "The parties to the marriage have lived apart for a continuous period of at least two years immediately preceding the presentation of the petition . . . and the respondent consents to a decree being granted."

To establish this ground it must be shown that there was separation for two years and that the parties consent. If the parties have separated but the other party refuses to consent then the petitioner must rely on one of the other grounds.

In some cases it has been troublesome to determine whether or not a couple are separate. In cases where the parties are living in separate houses the case will be straightforward, but the courts have acknowledged that parties can live separately under one roof. The courts will consider whether they were living communal lives and ask questions such as whether the couple ate together or helped in household tasks (*Santos v Santos* [1972]).

If they can show that even though living at the same address, they were living separate lives, the court will accept this can amount to a separation.

Five years separation

Key definition: five years separation

The Matrimonial Causes Act 1973, s 1(2)(e) defines five years separation as follows: "The parties to the marriage have lived apart for a continuous period of at least five years immediately preceding the presentation of the petition."

Notably for this ground there is no need for the respondent to consent. A blameless spouse can therefore be divorced against her wishes, but only if their partner is willing to wait five years.

FIERCE DEBATE

One of the major issues of disagreement over the law on divorce is the extent to which divorce should be fault-based or no-fault-based. In other words should a "blameless spouse" be able to be divorced against their wishes? To some a law that requires parties to make allegations of blame against each other only stokes up the fires of bitterness, which will inevitably exist at the end of a relationship. To others, the law should recognise that the end of a marriage is something serious and requires proof that the other party has behaved badly enough to entitle the parties to a divorce.

BARS TO DIVORCE

In most cases once one of the facts is shown there is little more the court needs to do and it can start the divorce proceedings. This will be by issuing a decree nisi, followed by a decree absolute if there is no objection to the divorce being granted. However, for a respondent seeking to avoid a divorce in rare cases one of the following bars may apply to prevent a court from granting a divorce:

1   You cannot petition for a divorce until you have been married for one year (Matrimonial Causes Act 1973, s 3(1). Remember that an application for annulment can be made immediately after a marriage. So if a person wishes to end the marriage within the first year they should consider whether there is a case for annulment. If not, they must wait the one year and then apply for a divorce.

2   If the petitioner is relying on the five-year ground and the respondent will suffer "grave financial or other hardship" if the divorce is granted and it would be wrong in all the circumstances to grant the divorce, then a bar under section 5 can be raised. This is very rarely used. If one party will suffer financially from the divorce the court can normally avoid that by making financial orders on divorce (see Chapter 6).

3   A special provision was enacted in s 12A Matrimonial Causes Act 1973 to deal with problems with religious divorces. If a party seeking a divorce refuses to provide the other party with the religious divorce then the court can refuse to give the legal divorce. This is designed to prevent the unfortunate scenario of a person being divorced in the eyes of the law, but still married in the eyes of their religion.

4   If one of the facts relying on separation is being used but the court feels that the financial arrangements on divorce are not fair or reasonable or the best in the circumstances, then the court can decline to grant a divorce until a suitable financial arrangement is made: s 10(2) Matrimonial Causes Act 1973.

5   In exceptional cases the court can refuse to grant a decree of divorce absolute if the court needs more time to consider the arrangements for the children.

KEY CASE ANALYSIS: *Archer v Archer* **[1999] 1 FLR 327 CA**

Background

- A 55-year-old consultant orthopaedic surgeon had few assets, but a large pension.
- His wife, age 54, argued against a divorce on the basis that should he predecease her as his ex-spouse she would not be entitled to a share in his pension and would suffer financially.

Principle established

It was held the wife's financial position could not be seen as "grave hardship". She had assets of nearly £300,000 and a reasonably sized house.

PROCEDURES

The law on divorce can only really be understood when the procedural rules are understood. In 1973 a "special procedure" was introduced. This means that if a divorce is undefended then there is no hearing. The judge will simply read the petition and assume that what is alleged is true. The petitioner does not need to prove that the events referred to in the petition are true. There is some evidence of couples inventing facts to put in the petition or more commonly agreeing what facts they are willing to make public to be put in the petition. It is probably quite rare for the petition to include the real reasons why the marriage has broken down. Only in cases of defended divorce will the couple need to appear before the judge and the petitioner introduce evidence. Defended divorces are very rare for two reasons. First, they are very expensive. Second, they are widely regarded by professionals as a waste of time. If your spouse wants to divorce you is it really sensible to force them to remain married to you? Professionals, and judges, will do all they can to dissuade someone from defending a divorce petition.

THE GOALS OF A DIVORCE LAW

What should a good divorce law try and do? Unusually we have a legislative answer to that question. In section 1 of the Family Law Act 1996, six principles are set down to guide the law on divorce. The goals of a divorce law are set out in Figure 4.1.

These principles are not without critics. Some people argue that the law should not seek to "save marriages" if the couple have decided to end the marriage. There is, however, a general agreement that the current law fails to achieve these goals. The fact that a person

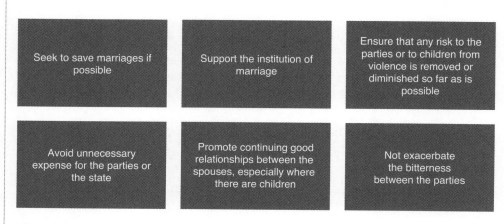

Figure 4.1 Goals of a divorce law

seeking a divorce without a lengthy period of separation is required to list in the petition the bad behaviour or adultery of the other party may be seen as being much more likely to produce bitterness than to avoid it.

FIERCE DEBATE

Should the law do more to save marriages? We could offer free marriage guidance counselling to all couples who apply for a divorce. Would that be a good idea? Some commentators believe so. They emphasise the harm that divorces can cause children and argue we have a duty to dissuade people from divorce. However, the majority view is that by the time the couple seek a divorce, the time for saving the marriage is long past. Indeed divorce is often sought because one party has decided they wish to remarry. By then it is far too late to try and achieve reconciliation. Perhaps providing marriage guidance more readily earlier in time would be more profitable than leaving it until the parties seek a divorce.

DISSOLUTION OF CIVIL PARTNERSHIPS

Divorce for same-sex couples is known as dissolution. The rules on civil partnership match those on marriage. So the ground for dissolution of a civil partnership is irretrievable breakdown. This must be proved by one of four facts. These are the same facts that can be used on divorce, save that adultery is not included. This is not as significant as might appear because in a case of sexual unfaithfulness that may well fall under the behaviour ground.

JUDICIAL SEPARATION

Sometimes a client will have a religious objection to marriage. Strict Roman Catholics, for example, are not permitted to divorce. If their relationship has broken down the court can offer a decree of **judicial separation**. This does not formally bring the marriage to an end. It is an acknowledgement that the parties have separated. Most importantly, it enables the courts to make financial orders relating to the couple (although not pension sharing orders), so that the long term financial futures of the couple can be arranged.

REFORMS

There is a widespread feeling that the law on divorce should be reformed. Here we will consider two proposals.

Family Justice Act 1996

The Family Justice Act 1996 proposed reform of the divorce law, but this was never implemented, after unsuccessful pilot studies. The proposal was that a party seeking to divorce would initiate the divorce process by attending an "information meeting", which would inform about the divorce process and the availability of marriage guidance. After a period of reflection the party could file a statement of marital breakdown. There would then follow a period of reflection and consideration when the parties would consider whether they really wanted divorce and if so what the financial arrangements and those for the children should be. The total length of the process from its start to when the divorce order could be made was 12 months and 14 days for those without children and 18 months and 14 days for those with children.

A number of features of this proposal are interesting. First, the proposal does away with the requirement of making allegations of fault. Second, an explicit aim of the proposal was to encourage the parties to think carefully about whether or not they wanted a divorce and to encourage them to save their marriage through marriage guidance. The pilot studies found very few marriages were saved. This is perhaps not surprising. People turn to the law when the relationship has completely broken down (and often when they wish to remarry) and so the time for marriage guidance is long past. Third, the process takes a long time. To many commentators this was a major disadvantage of the process.

FIERCE DEBATE

Do you think the law should do more to encourage people seeking a divorce to take time to think through the issues? How would you feel if you sought a divorce and were told to spend time making sure you had made the right decision? One interesting idea is that rather than requiring a waiting period before a divorce we should have a waiting period before marriage!

Family Justice Review

A more recent proposal to reform the law can be found in the Family Justice Review of 2012. This proposed that those seeking a divorce could go online and access an "information hub" with a "divorce portal". An online form for divorce would be available and this would be dealt with by a court processing centre. If the other party did not object, a court officer could automatically produce a divorce. Notably the procedure did not suggest that the grounds for divorce be changed, but that the procedure would be cheaper because it would not involve judges or lawyers and could be done online.

This proposal is openly focussed on saving costs. If enacted it would be likely to do this. Some may believe that moving to "divorce by internet" trivialises divorce. However, this may be old fashioned. All kinds of significant transactions are undertaken by internet and maybe having a cheap and efficient system is important.

On-the-spot question

In America some states allow couples who are marrying to choose between a normal marriage and a "covenant marriage". With a normal marriage the couple can divorce if either of them wish the marriage to end. However, with a covenant marriage the marriage can only be ended if the other party has behaved in a particularly bad way. Would that be a good reform? What kind of marriage would you choose?

SUMMARY

- The ground for divorce or dissolution is that the marriage or civil partnership has irretrievably broken down.
- Irretrievable breakdown can only be established by proving one of the facts listed in the statute (e.g. adultery; unreasonable behaviour).
- Very rarely a bar to divorce can arise, even where one of the facts is proved.
- There have been repeated calls for reform of the law on divorce.

FURTHER READING

R Deech, "Divorce: A disaster" (2009) 39 *Family Law* 1048 – argues that the law needs to do more to deter and prevent divorce.

J Herring, "Divorce, internet hubs and Stephen Cretney" in R Probert and C Barton (eds) *Fifty Years in Family Law* (Intersentia, 2012) – discusses the proposals for the reform of divorce in the Family Justice Review.

H Reece, *Divorcing Responsibly* (Hart, 2003) – discusses the role the state should play in divorce.

J Shepherd, "Ending the blame game: Getting no fault divorce back on the agenda" (2009) *Family Law* 122 – discusses the need to remove fault from the divorce system.

Chapter 5
Domestic abuse

LEARNING OBJECTIVES

After reading this chapter you should be able to:

- understand the definition and nature of domestic violence;
- be able to explain the civil law remedies to domestic abuse;
- consider the response of the criminal law to domestic abuse;
- explain the difficulties the law faces in responding to domestic abuse.

INTRODUCTION

Domestic violence is a major social problem. About one in three women will suffer domestic abuse at some point in their life. And about one in six men will. The law has been slow to respond to the issue, which until relatively recently has been ignored. Indeed it was not until 1991 that it was held that a husband could be convicted of raping his wife (*R v R*).

At one time domestic violence was seen as a private matter that was best left to the couple to resolve between themselves. It was thought that the state and police had the job of keeping peace in public places, such as roads and parks, but that it was not their business to keep the peace in people's home. That attitude has few supporters today. It is recognised there is a significant social impact from domestic violence and it cannot be categorised as straightforwardly a private matter.

THE DEFINITION OF DOMESTIC VIOLENCE

Key definition: domestic violence

Legal Aid, Sentencing and Punishment of Offenders Act 2012, Sch 1 (as amended) reads:

> "Domestic violence" means any incident, or pattern of incidents, of controlling, coercive or threatening behaviour, violence or abuse (whether psychological, physical, sexual, financial or emotional) between individuals who are associated with each other.

The Government has expanded on this:

> Any incident or pattern of incidents of controlling, coercive or threatening behaviour, violence or abuse between those aged 16 or over who are or have been intimate partners or family members regardless of gender or sexuality. This can encompass, but is not limited to, the following types of abuse:
>
> - psychological
> - physical
> - sexual
> - financial
> - emotional
>
> Controlling behaviour is: a range of acts designed to make a person subordinate and/or dependent by isolating them from sources of support, exploiting their resources and capacities for personal gain, depriving them of the means needed for independence, resistance and escape and regulating their everyday behaviour.
>
> Coercive behaviour is: an act or a pattern of acts of assault, threats, humiliation and intimidation or other abuse that is used to harm, punish, or frighten their victim.

There are two things to notice about the definition of domestic violence in the Legal Aid, Sentencing and Punishment of Offenders Act 2012. First, domestic violence is understood as a course of conduct rather than an isolated event. This is helpful because it emphasises the importance of understanding each act in the context of the relationship. An act that may appear relatively minor, may in fact be a part of a highly abusive relationship. Second, domestic violence is seen as being about gaining control of the other party. This may involve acts of violence, but can also include control by emotional or threatening behaviour. Perhaps this is a more controversial suggestion, as it suggests that a single act of violence, which is not part of a relationship that is generally a controlling one, might not fall full squarely into the definition of domestic violence.

KEY CASE ANALYSIS: *Yemshaw v London Borough of Hounslow* [2011] UKSC 3

Background

- Mrs Yemshaw sought housing from the local authority under the Housing Act 1996.
- To be entitled to housing she had to show she was the victim of domestic violence.
- She accepted her husband had not been physically violent but said he had been threatening and emotionally abusive.

Principle established

Domestic violence should be understood in a broad sense in this context. It was not restricted to cases of physical assault and could include putting someone in fear of violence; denigrating a person's personality or depriving someone of their liberty.

REAL WORLD

Around one in three women and nearly one in five men have experienced domestic abuse by a partner or family member since the age of 16. Every six minutes on average, as least one killing, stabbing or beating takes place in Britain. Of all violent crime committed, 18 per cent is domestic violence.

CIVIL ORDERS

One set of legal remedies available for a victim of domestic violence is to seek a civil order. The applicant will have to apply to the court for the order. There are three kinds of orders they may seek, as shown in Figure 5.1.

Figure 5.1 Civil domestic violence orders

Non-molestation order

Key definition: molestation

Acts that threaten or harass the victim. There is no need for physical violence but the acts must involve more than an invasion of privacy.

Non-molestation orders can be sought under s 42 Family Law Act 1996. In deciding whether or not to make a non-molestation order, the court will take all the circumstances of the case into account, in particular the health, safety and well-being of the applicant and any children. A non-molestation order will require the respondent to stop molesting the applicant. It can identify particular acts that are prohibited. For example, the order may prohibit the respondent from texting the applicant or from going to her place of work.

In order to apply for a non-molestation order the applicant must be associated with the respondent.

Key definition: associated people

There are eight categories of associated people, defined in detail in section 62 Family Law Act 1996:

1   They are, or have been, either civil partners or married to each other.
2   They are cohabitants or former cohabitants.
3   They have, or have had, an intimate personal relationship with each other, which is or was of a significant duration.

4   They live, or have lived, in the same household, otherwise than merely by reason of one of them being the other's employee, tenant, lodger or boarder.

5   They are relatives. This is given a very wide definition in s 63(1) and even includes nephews, nieces and cousins.

6   They have agreed to marry one another or enter a civil partnership (whether or not that agreement has been terminated).

7   In relation to any child, a parent of a child or someone who has parental responsibility for the child.

8   They are parties to the same family proceedings in court.

This is a notably broad list. It includes people who are in a close relationship, even if they are not living together. Note it does not include couples who are going out together, but are not cohabiting nor having a sexual relationship. Nor does it include a stalking case if the victim has never been in a relationship with the stalker. In such cases, where the two parties are not associated the Protection from Harassment Act 1997 should be used.

On-the-spot question

Is the list of associated people too broad? It includes a niece or nephew, for example? If domestic violence is about a controlling relationship, should the list be restricted to those who actually share a house? Or is the definition a welcome acknowledgement that one person can control another even though they are not living together?

Breach of a non-molestation order

Breach of a non-molestation order is a criminal offence under s 42A Family Law Act 1996. There is, however, a defence if the defendant had a reasonable excuse. For example, if a non-molestation order forbade the defendant from contacting the victim, but he phoned her to pass on news that a relative had died, the court might accept that the breach was reasonable. There is also a defence if the defendant was not aware that the non-molestation order was made. There is a maximum sentence of five years.

Occupation orders

Occupation orders are designed to remove someone from parts of the home, all of the home, or even an area around the home. It is therefore much more dramatic than a non-molestation order. It should not be surprising to learn that occupation orders are harder to obtain than non-molestation orders.

The law on occupation orders is somewhat complex. There are four different sections and Table 5.1 shows who should use which section.

Table 5.1 Family Law Act occupation orders

Section number	Who for?
33	Spouse, ex-spouse, civil partner, or holder of property right
36	Cohabitant or former cohabitant without property interest (where respondent has a property interest)
37	Ex-spouse or ex-civil partner without a property interest
38	Cohabitants where neither party has a property interest

Section 33 orders

Most cases will be brought under section 33. This can be used by any applicant who has a property interest and is associated with the respondent, and by current or former spouses or civil partners. To know if the applicant has a property interest or not the general law on property will be used, discussed in Chapter 4.

In any case brought under section 33 the starting point is the significant harm test set out under s 33(8). The court must consider two scenarios:

1   What will happen if no order is made? Will the applicant or any relevant child suffer significant harm attributable to the conduct of the respondent?
2   What will happen if an order is made? Will the respondent or any relevant child suffer significant harm?

Section 33(8) states that if the judge determines that without an order the applicant or child will suffer significant harm (scenario 1) and that that harm will be more than the respondent or child will suffer if the order is made (scenario 2), then the court must make an order. However, if that is not so, the court is still permitted to make an order; it is just that it does not have to (*Chalmers v Johns* [1998]). The court must then consider the general factors in section 33(6) (see Figure 5.2).

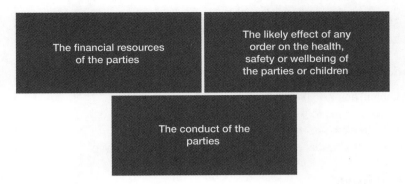

Figure 5.2 The general grounds

The following cases give you a good idea of how the courts have interpreted the balance of harm test and the kind of cases where an occupation order may be appropriate.

KEY CASE ANALYSIS: *Chalmers v Johns* **[1998] EWCA Civ 1452**

Background

- The cohabiting parties had a difficult relationship.
- There had been violence against each other and minor injuries had resulted.
- The woman moved out of the house with her daughter into temporary council accommodation.

Principle established

- The Court of Appeal refused to make an occupation order. There was no significant harm that was likely to befall the woman.
- The child was not at risk of harm. The claim the child had a long walk to school was not one that could amount to significant harm.
- An occupation order should be regarded as exceptional and draconian.
- Any difficulties the mother and daughter faced could be dealt with by other orders short of removing the father from his house.

KEY CASE ANALYSIS: *B v B (Occupation Order)* [1999] 1 FLR 715

Background

- The husband and wife had been living in a council house.
- The mother left and took the baby with her.
- The husband remained in the home with his six-year-old son.
- It was found the husband had been extremely violent to the wife.

Principle established

- The wife and baby were living in inadequate accommodation and that was seen as constituting significant harm.
- However, if the order were made the husband and son would need to move and there was no appropriate accommodation for them.
- Balancing the harms, the harm to the son especially, was greater than that faced by the mother and baby. This meant it was not appropriate for an order to be made.

KEY CASE ANALYSIS: *Re Y (Children)(Occupation Order)* [2000] 2 FCR 470

Background

- The marriage had broken down.
- There was constant shouting and arguing in the house.
- One child sided with the wife and the other the father.

Principle

- An occupation order should not be made except as a "last resort" in "exceptional cases".
- Removing someone from their home was a "draconian order".
- Here the atmosphere in the house was unpleasant but no more than the "ordinary tensions of divorce".

KEY CASE ANALYSIS: *Grubb v Grubb* [2009] EWCA Civ 976

Background

- The husband and wife were divorcing.
- The husband excluded the wife from the house and took her keys.
- She sought an occupation order.

Principle established

- In this case the relationship had broken down and it was clear the parties could not live in the same house.
- The key feature was the availability of alternative accommodation. The husband had ready access to another place to live and plenty of money, while the wife did not.
- The occupation order removing the husband should be made.

KEY CASE ANALYSIS: *Dolan v Corby* [2011] EWCA 1664

Background

- The parties were cohabiting as joint tenants of a home they had lived in for thirty years.
- There was evidence of verbal abuse from the respondent.
- The applicant had psychiatric problems.

Principle established

- An occupation order could be made even though there had not been violence.
- The psychiatric state of the applicant meant it was harder for her to find accommodation than the respondent.
- This meant the order was appropriate.

KEY CASE ANALYSIS: *Re L (Children)* **[2012] EWCA cv 721**

Background

- The couple had heated rows, although it was not found there had been serious violence.
- The husband was removed from the house under an occupation order.

Principle established

The harm to the children of witnessing the rows was a sufficiently good reason to justify the order. They were in danger of suffering further emotional harm without an order.

Several points emerge from these cases. The first is that removing someone from their home is seen as "draconian" or "serious". This means that the courts will require some kind of significant or unusual harm before an order will be made. The second is that the courts will focus on the needs of the parties more than who is to blame. A party who needs accommodation may obtain an occupation order, even though the other party has not behaved in a particularly serious way. Finally, the occupation order is seen as a matter of last resort. If there are other ways of resolving the problems the couple face, short of a housing order, the courts will prefer that.

FIERCE DEBATE

Should the conduct of the parties play a greater role in civil orders? The Law Commission suggested that the courts should focus on the needs of the parties and not consider their blameworthiness or otherwise. However, the Act does mention the conduct of the parties, but only as a factor to consider. Indeed it would not be impossible for the courts to order the "victim" of the domestic violence to leave if she had good alternative accommodation to go to.

The courts have a wide range of powers for applicants under section 33. These may involve allowing the applicant to remain in occupation; requiring the respondent to leave the house; allowing the applicant to enter in the house; regulating the occupation (e.g. by not allowing the respondent into certain rooms of the house or only allowing the respondent to enter at certain times of the day); and removing the respondent from the house and even a defined area around the house.

Section 35 orders

Section 35 deals with ex-spouses or ex-civil partners who have no right to occupy and it has similar provisions to those for section 33. The primary difference is that the balance of harm test does not apply. Although the questions in the balance of harm test must be asked (what will happen if an order is made? What will happen if an order is not made?) they do not require the court to make a particular order based on the answers. Rather the courts must take them into account together with the "general factors" listed above, and some additional factors, including the length of time since the marriage or civil partnership came to an end. Presumably if it has been some time since the divorce or dissolution it will be hard to justify making an order.

Orders under sections 36, 37 and 38

For sections 36, 37 and 38 the significant harm test does not apply. This will make it harder for an applicant under these sections to obtain an occupation order than it is for an applicant under section 33. Further, the range of orders is more limited and only provides temporary assistance.

On-the-spot question

Notice that married couples automatically fall within the favoured section 33, while cohabitants need to establish a property interest to do so. Should it really matter in cases of domestic violence whether the parties are married or not? In the debates before the legislation some MPs suggested treating married and unmarried couples in the same way undermined the status of marriage. Would you agree?

Protection from Harassment Act 1997

Civil orders are also available under the Protection from Harassment Act 1997. Significantly this Act can be used by anyone. There is no need to show the parties are related or were in a serious relationship. It is, therefore, particularly useful in cases where a person is being stalked by a stranger. To use the legislation it must be shown that there has been a course of conduct that amounts to harassment and which the person knows or ought to know amounts to harassment. There is an aggravated version of the offence under section 4, which involves a course of conduct that causes a person to fear on at least two occasions that violence will be used against them.

There are defences in the Act. Most notably that the course of conduct was reasonable. So a person who writes several letters asking for payment of a debt is likely to be found to be acting reasonably.

Breach of the 1997 Act can also give rise to a payment of damages and the court can award an injunction restricting someone from engaging in conduct that amounts to harassment.

KEY CASE ANALYSIS: *Lau v DPP* **[2000] 1 FLR 799**

Background

- The defendant slapped his girlfriend.
- Four months later he was verbally abusive to her in the street.

Principle established

- He had not committed "harassment" under the 1997 Act.
- Although there were two pieces of conduct, to be a course of conduct they had to be connected.
- Here there was insufficient nexus between the incidents.
- There was a significant gap in time between them and they were different in nature.

KEY CASE ANALYSIS: *R v Hills* **[2001] FLR 580**

Background

- The defendant had assaulted his cohabitant in two separate assaults, six months apart, and was convicted under the Protection from Harassment Act 1997.
- He appealed, claiming that there was no course of conduct because the couple had reconciled in between the two incidents.

Principle established

- The Court of Appeal held that the Protection from Harassment Act 1997 was particularly designed to deal with stalking cases.

- In this case, where the couple had reconciled, lived together and had sexual intercourse, this was too far away from the stalking paradigm to amount to a course of conduct.
- The further apart the pieces of conduct the less likely it was that they would be regarded as a course of conduct.

KEY CASE ANALYSIS: *R v Widdows* [2011] EWCA 1500

Background

- The defendant and victim had a "mature" but "volatile" relationship.
- There were frequent rows, acts of violence, separations and reconciliations.
- The man was charged with aggravated harassment, under section 4 of the Act.

Principle established

- The Court of Appeal held that the term harassment implied "stalkers, racial abusers, disruptive neighbours, bullying at work and so forth".
- The relationship here was outside the kind of cases that were at the heart of the Act.
- The couple were by and large together during the period of the relevant incidents.
- The defendant could be charged with assaults for any individual acts, but they did not fall within a course of conduct.

STALKING

Section 2A of the Protection from Harassment Act 1997 has a specific offence of stalking. It involves a course of conduct that amounts to harassment and is stalking.

Key definition: stalking

The 1997 Act does not define stalking, but it gives a long list of examples of behaviour "associated with stalking":

(3)   The following are examples of acts or omissions which, in particular circumstances, are ones associated with stalking–

(a)   following a person,

(b)   contacting, or attempting to contact, a person by any means,

(c)   publishing any statement or other material–

(i)   relating or purporting to relate to a person, or

(ii)   purporting to originate from a person,

(d)   monitoring the use by a person of the internet, email or any other form of electronic communication,

(e)   loitering in any place (whether public or private),

(f)   interfering with any property in the possession of a person,

(g)   watching or spying on a person.

CRIMINAL LAW

The normal criminal law applies to domestic violence. Just because an assault takes place in a home does not make it any less of a criminal offence than if it had taken place in the street. In *R v R* [1991] it was confirmed that the rule that used to state that a husband could not be convicted of raping his wife had been abolished.

There are some additional provisions for domestic violence cases. Under the Crime and Security Act 2010 a police officer can issue a domestic violence protection notice, if she believes that someone has been the victim of domestic violence and that issuing the notice will protect them. If that notice is breached then a domestic violence protection order can be made.

FIERCE DEBATE

There has been much consideration over what should happen if the police believe a domestic assault has taken place but the victim does not want a prosecution to take place. Some believe that the victim should be allowed to control the prosecution and that it should only take place with her consent. There are practical reasons for this, namely that it will be difficult to prove a crime has occurred if the victim is not willing to give evidence about it. There are also principled reasons, namely that the victim's autonomy should be respected and it would be paternalistic to prosecute against her wishes.

Others disagree and argue that a prosecution is brought by the state not the victim, that domestic violence causes serious social harms and we need to discourage it and so a prosecution is appropriate even where the victim opposes it. Further, if the victim opposes a prosecution this may be because they are fearful, rather than these being their genuine wishes.

SUMMARY

- Domestic violence is understood to be acts that constitute acts that create a controlling relationship.
- Violent incidents of domestic violence can be treated as crimes and prosecuted by the police.
- There are civil orders available, which can offer protection to the victim of domestic violence.
- The civil orders include those that require one party to vacate the property or to stop molesting the other.

FURTHER READING

M Burton, *Legal Responses to Domestic Violence* (Routledge, 2008) – examines the law on domestic violence.

S Choudhry and J Herring, "Righting domestic violence" (2006) 20 *International Journal of Law, Policy and the Family* 95 – argues that the law should take account of human rights in domestic violence law.

J Herring, "The meaning of domestic violence" (2011) *Journal of Social Welfare and Family Law* 297 – considers the definition of domestic violence.

M Hester, "The three planet model: Towards an understanding of contradictions in approaches to women and children's safety in contexts of domestic violence" (2011) 41 *British Journal of Social Work* 837 – considers domestic violence in the broader context of family law.

M Madden Dempsey, *Prosecuting Domestic Violence* (Oxford University Press, 2009) – examines when criminal prosecutions for domestic violence should take place.

Chapter 6
Financial orders on separation

LEARNING OBJECTIVES

After reading this chapter you should be able to:

- understand the statutory provisions relating to financial orders;
- be able to explain the case law on financial orders;
- discuss the theoretical issues around financial orders;
- explore the law on child support.

INTRODUCTION

For many married couples or those in a civil partnership the question of who owns what property does not come up. They share their assets and lives without question. However, on divorce or dissolution the issue can become a major one. This is particularly true because during a marriage or civil partnership there can be financial gains and losses for the parties, looked at as individuals. Traditionally, for example, a wife might give up a career to look after children and suffer a financial loss as a result. While her husband's career may have blossomed and he has made a financial gain, her career has not developed at all and she may find it hard to re-enter the employment market. Where the economic losses and gains have not been shared equally during the marriage then it seems only fair that the law should ensure that on divorce there is a fair sharing of the benefits and disadvantages of the marriage. That is what the court seeks to do with financial orders at the end of the marriage.

Before looking further at this issue it is crucial to appreciate there is a huge difference between the powers of the courts when a court deals with the end of a marriage or civil partnership and a case involving a couple who are simply living together. Where the couple are living together outside marriage or civil partnership the court has no power to order one party to transfer property to the other or to pay ongoing maintenance. However, if the couple are married or in a civil partnership, the court has the power, in theory at least, to require one party to give the other everything they own.

REAL WORLD

A leading study in the UK on the impact of divorce states:

> The stark conclusion is that men's household income increases by about 23 per cent on divorce once we control for household size, whereas women's household income falls by about 31 per cent. There is partial recovery for women, but this recovery is driven by re-partnering: the average effect of re-partnering is to restore income to pre-divorce levels after nine years.

FINANCIAL ORDERS ON MARRIAGE

The following orders are available on divorce or dissolutions:

1   **A periodic payments order.** This is an order that one spouse pay the other monthly (or weekly) payments. It is possible to put a time limit on the order. So, for example, a husband may be ordered to pay his ex-wife £100 a month for the next three years.
2   **Property adjustment order.** This is an order that one person transfer ownership of property into another's name. Most commonly this will be the house. So a court may require a wife to transfer ownership of a house in her husband's name so he can live there with the children.
3   **Lump sum order.** This is an order that a specified sum of money be paid by one spouse to another. For example, a husband may be required to pay £10,000 to his wife.
4   **Pension sharing order.** This is an order that one person's pension be divided into two. This is likely to be used where one spouse has through their employment got a large pension and the other because of their family responsibilities has no pension provision.

FACTORS TO BE TAKEN INTO ACCOUNT

Section 25(2) of the Matrimonial Causes Act 1973 lists nine factors that a court should take into account when deciding what order, if any, to make on divorce:

1   The first consideration is to be "the welfare while a minor of any child of the family who has not reached the age of 18".

The court will want to start by ensuring that the needs of the children are met. Sometimes the needs of the children are such that there is no money left to divide between the adults (*B v B (Financial Provision)* [2002]).

2 "The income, earning capacity, property and other financial resources which each of the parties to the marriage has or is likely to have in the foreseeable future, including in the case of earning capacity any increase in that capacity which it would in the opinion of the court be reasonable to expect a party to the marriage to take steps to acquire."

It is obvious that the assets that the parties have will be a key feature. If one spouse has a large proportion of assets and the other party has nothing, it is likely the court will want to make the position more equal. However, there are some interesting features to notice about the wording of this provision.

First, the court is required to consider a person's earning capacity. This might be relevant in a case where, say, a wife claims that she has helped her husband get into a position where he can earn a large salary. In *Parlour v Parlour* [2004] a wife claimed she had helped her husband rebuild his football career so that he was now an international footballer and could expect a huge salary in the years ahead. She claimed she should be entitled to a share in his future income because it was due to her efforts in the marriage that he was in the position of earning a large salary. It may also be relevant in a case where a spouse has not worked during the marriage, but the other spouse claims they could easily put themselves into a position where they had a well-paid job. So, if a wife claimed she had substantial needs and no income because she had cared for the children during the marriage, the husband may well reply that the wife had the capacity to earn a substantial salary. The court might not expect a parent caring for very young children or a disabled child to work, but once the children are at school a judge may well expect both parents to work unless there are good reasons why not.

Second, the provision relates to financial resources a party is likely to receive in the future. This will include a pension payment to which a party might be entitled in the future. The courts tend to focus on sums that a spouse will definitely obtain. So the fact the husband has a rich aunt who might leave him a fortune in the future will probably not be considered because that would be too speculative.

Third, all assets of the parties are to be considered. This can include income unrelated to the marriage, such as a lottery win (*S v AG (Financial Order Lottery Prize)* [2011]). As we shall see later, in big money cases the courts may pay some attention to whether the property was generated during the marriage, but for most divorces that is not a relevant issue.

Fourth, there has been some dispute over whether a new partner's income was relevant. The law is clear that when a party remarries their first spouse is no longer required to pay financial support for them. But the issue is less clear if the spouse simply cohabits with someone. The following case offers some guidance.

KEY CASE ANALYSIS: *Grey v Grey* [2010] EWCA Civ 1424

Background

- A husband was paying his ex-wife financial support.
- He claimed that his wife's new long-term partner could be contributing to his wife's needs.

Principle established

- The Court of Appeal agreed. It rejected an argument that the husband should not be liable at all to support his ex-wife if she had a new partner.
- However, it was necessary to look at the new partner's ability to contribute to her needs.
- Indeed when the case was reheard (*Re Grey* (no 3) [2010] EWHC 1055 (Fam)) the husband's contribution was reduced.

---

3   "The financial needs, obligations and responsibilities, which each of the parties to the marriage has or is likely to have in the foreseeable future."

The previous factor looked at the assets of the parties. This one focuses on their needs. It is worth emphasising that there is no restriction on the needs in question. They do not need to relate to the marriage itself. So, if a spouse's parent is in a nursing home and there are expensive costs these may be taken into account even though they arose separately from the marriage. The same would be true of debts that a party had before a marriage and they still had at the end.

A controversial issue has been the extent to which responsibilities for a new family can be taken into account. If, for example, a husband has left his wife and moved in with a woman who has children, can he say that his obligations to his new family mean he has fewer resources available to support his ex-wife? The courts have not produced a consistent view on this (contrast *S v S (Financial Provision: Departing from Equality)* [2001] and *H-J v H-J (Financial Provision: Equality)* [2002]). The general view seems to be that in such a case a husband cannot diminish his responsibilities to his first wife by choosing to take on new obligations.

4   "The standard of living enjoyed by the family before the breakdown of the marriage."

This factor is taken into account when the courts assess the needs of the party. If, for example, a woman married a very rich man and enjoyed a luxurious lifestyle she might expect to continue living at a similar standard of living after the marriage has broken down. Assuming he has a lot of money she might expect to live in a large house and have a nice car. However, sometimes this factor can limit a claim. In *K v L* [2011] the wife was very wealthy but the couple during their marriage lived in a very modest way. This was held as a reason for restricting the husband's claim to a relatively modest one. He could expect to continue to live at the level they enjoyed during the marriage, but not at an enhanced one.

5   "The age of each party to the marriage and the duration of the marriage."

The age of the parties is unlikely to be particularly relevant, except as evidence about their needs or expected income in the future. So, the fact one party is close to retirement is clearly a relevant factor. The length of the marriage is a more significant factor. Where the marriage has been very short the court will be tempted to put the parties back in the position they were in before they were married. The longer the marriage the stronger the argument will be that the couple should share all the assets.

One issue that the courts have addressed under this heading is whether the court can consider the length of the marriage or whether it can take into account the pre-marital calculation. Originally the courts said that only the actual marriage would be considered, but now the court will take into account the total length of the relationship.

6   "Any physical or mental disability of either of the parties to the marriage."

This factor emphasises the importance of looking at the needs of the parties. In *C v C (Financial Provision: Personal Damages)* [1997] a husband who was severely disabled was left with £5 million, which he needed to meet his care and medical needs, while the wife was left with virtually nothing. This shows how the needs of the parties may mean that one spouse receives a far larger share of the couple's finances than the other.

7   "The contributions which each of the parties has made or is likely in the foreseeable future to make to the welfare of the family, including any contribution by looking after the home or caring for the family."

This important provision has been interested by the House of Lords in *White v White* [2000]. There it was said that the court would regard the contribution to a marriage through child care or home making as of equal value as economic contribution. So the courts will give no truck to an argument "I worked hard to make the money so I should keep it all". Indeed generally the courts are reluctant to rely on this subsection to consider whether one party contributed more to the marriage than the other. However, the future contributions to caring for the family are relevant. If one spouse is going to take on the primary role of caring for the children after the marriage, this will clearly have an impact on their ability to provide for themselves financially.

8   "The conduct of the parties, if that conduct is such that it would in the opinion of the court be inequitable to disregard it."

At one time the conduct of the parties was a key factor and a party who behaved badly could expect to have any award severely reduced. However, nowadays it is rare for conduct to be taken into account. In *Miller* the House of Lords thought the husband's adultery was not a factor on its own to be considered to enhance the award to the wife. Interestingly the Court of Appeal in that case had used the adultery to increase the award. As a result of this decision it is clear that only in more extreme circumstances will the conduct of the parties be a relevant factor. In *H v H (Financial Relief: Attempted Murder as Conduct)* [2006] the husband's attempted murder of the wife was held to be a relevant factor. But the very fact this case was heard on appeal is an indication that the issue was debatable and how high the bar has been set for conduct to be sufficiently serious to be relevant. In *K v L* [2010] the sexual abuse by the husband of grandchildren was a factor to take into account.

The courts seem more willing to take conduct into account where it is financial and has had an impact on the couple's finances. In *H v H (Financial Provision: Conduct)* [1998] a husband had transferred money from the couple's account to an account in Switzerland in his own name, without his wife's knowledge. That was a relevant factor in deciding to enhance the award to the wife. Similarly where a spouse has wasted assets through gambling or excessive spending that might, in some cases, be considered.

FIERCE DEBATE

Should the law take more account of the fault of the parties? If the husband has run off with a younger woman should he pay his ex-spouse more than if he was not at fault? If we did a poll of the public a majority may well support penalising cheating spouses in this way. Is that a good reason for doing so?

9   "The value to each of the parties to the marriage of any benefits, which, by reason of the dissolution or annulment of the marriage, that party will lose the chance of acquiring."

This is most relevant in the court determining whether to make a pension sharing order. Sometimes the court will decide not to split a pension but instead give one party a lump sum instead.

Applying the factors

This long list of factors can seem rather daunting. How can a judge weigh up all these competing factors? In fact in most cases there is very little a judge can do. The couple, at least by the time of the divorce, will have no money or very little. The little there is will be used to meet the needs of the children and perhaps ensure they have a home to live in, but factors beyond the basic needs of parties pale into insignificance. This is especially true given the extent to which many, even middle-class families, have substantial mortgages and debts and are barely able to service one household, yet alone the two that will exist on divorce. The only cases where there is really very much redistribution that the courts can do are the cases that involve the very rich. Perhaps unsurprisingly it is these which make up the vast majority of cases.

BIG MONEY CASES

In recent years the courts have developed a particular approach to big money cases, based on three leading cases.

KEY CASE ANALYSIS: *White v White* [2000] 3 FCR 555

Background

- Mr and Mrs White had been married for 33 years.
- Their assets were £4.5 million from a farm they had run together, although Mrs White was also involved in caring for the children.
- At first instance the judge made an order to meet her needs, at somewhat under a million pounds.

Principle established

- Fairness was to be the primary objective in financial orders. That required the court to ensure the primary needs of the couple were met.
- If, as in this case, there were more than enough assets to meet the needs of the parties, the court should use the "yardstick of equality".
- The court would presume that a couple had contributed equally to a marriage and no distinction would be drawn between contributions of child care or home making and economic contributions. Therefore their assets should be divided equally.

- In some cases there would be a good reason to depart from equality. There was in this case because the farms had been brought with money provided by the husband's family.
- Mrs White was awarded 40 per cent of the total assets.

KEY CASE ANALYSIS: *Miller v Miller* [2006] 2 FCR 213

Background

- A couple were married for three years.
- The husband had an affair with a younger woman and this ended the marriage.
- The husband was worth over £17 million at the date of divorce.

Principle established

- The adultery was not conduct such that it was inequitable to disregard.
- The wife was entitled to a half share of the assets under the *White* principle, but only half of the assets generated during the marriage. That was because it was a short marriage. In a long marriage it may be fair to divide all assets.
- Fortunately for Mrs Miller her husband had been financially very successful during the marriage and she was entitled to £5 million.

KEY CASE ANALYSIS: *McFarlane v McFarlane* [2006] 2 FCR 213

Background

- The couple had been married for 16 years and had three children.
- When they married the couple both had successful careers. But the wife gave up her job to care for the children and had not been employed for most of the marriage.
- The couple had £3 million of assets and the husband earned £750,000 per year.

Principle

- The starting point, given the length of the marriage was a division of the capital. However in this case that would not produce a fair result.
- If each party left the marriage with £1.5 million, but the husband earned £750,000 per year and the wife nothing, this would not provide the wife with appropriate compensation for the fact that she had lost her earning potential during the marriage.
- The husband was required to make sizeable annual payments to the wife in addition.

These cases have led to the emergence of a relatively consistent approach in big money cases. The guiding criterion in all cases is achieving fairness. The court will look at three factors in particular:

1 Needs. The needs of the party will take into account the kind of lifestyle they enjoyed during the marriage.
2 Sharing. In the case of short marriages only the assets generated during the marriage will be shared, while in long marriages all the assets the couple have will be taken into account. The court will always consider whether there are good reasons to depart from equal sharing. This can include where one party had inherited money (*K v L* [2011]) or, occasionally, where one party had made an outstanding contribution to the marriage (*Sorrell v Sorrell* [2006]).
3 Compensation. The court will ensure that if possible a party is compensated for any losses (including lost earning potential) caused by the marriage.

In applying these principles no difference will be drawn between an opposite-sex couple and a same-sex couple or between a marriage and a civil partnership.

These principles were applied in one famous divorce.

KEY CASE ANALYSIS: *McCartney v Mills McCartney* [2008] FCR 708

Background

- Paul McCartney married Heather Mills in 2002 and divorced four years later.
- They had one child.
- McCartney's wealth was said to be £400 million.

Principle established

- The marriage was short and so only the assets generated during the marriage were to be divided.
- However, McCartney had largely taken a break from economic ventures during the marriage and so there was negligible income relating to the marriage.
- Mills could not claim compensation as it had not been shown the marriage damaged her earning potential; indeed if anything it enhanced it.
- This left only needs as the basis for an award. £16.5 million was sufficient to meet her needs and those of the daughter.

On-the-spot question

Do you think it right that a rich spouse should have to share their assets on divorce? Are the courts paying too much attention to the idea of gender equality? Or are the courts right to insist that a contribution to a marriage through child care is as valuable as a financial contribution?

CLEAN BREAKS

The courts generally wish to create a clean break.

Key definition: clean break

A clean break is a financial order which means there is no on going financial responsibility between the parties. It is a "once and for all" order which means no further payments or orders will be required.

Typically in a clean break order one party will pay the other a lump sum of money or transfer a piece of property and that will satisfy any financial obligations owed. Baroness Hale has summarised the benefits of a clean break order (*Miller v Miller* [2006]):

Periodical payments are a continuing source of stress for both parties. They are also insecure. With the best will in the world, the paying party may fall on hard times and be unable to keep up with them . . . It is also the logical consequence of the retreat from the principle of the life-long obligation. Independent finances and self-sufficiency are the aims.

The courts are, therefore, seeking to avoid a situation where, say, a husband is paying his wife monthly sums for decades after a marriage has broken down. Even if an immediate clean break is possible the court may consider a "delayed clean break" (Matrimonial Causes Act 1973, s 25A(2)). That is an order that there be periodic payments but they are for a fixed length of time, say two years. This might be appropriate in a case where a spouse has not been working during the marriage and will need some time to get themselves in a position to find work. They will be given financial support for the next two years, but they know that by then they will be expected to be financially independent.

FIERCE DEBATE

Do you think a spouse should ever be responsible to their former spouse for years after a divorce? On the one side of the argument it might be said that the parties should be encouraged to become self-sufficient as soon as possible after the marriage. The days when marriage was a "meal ticket for life" should be long over. On the other hand it can be argued that the financial effects of marriage can be felt for decades afterwards. This might certainly be the case where a spouse is, say, caring for a disabled child. But it might also be where a spouse in middle age is left with no career prospects as a result of the care provided during the marriage.

PRE-NUPTIAL AGREEMENTS

Key definition: pre-nuptial agreement

A pre-nuptial agreement, sometimes called 'a pre-nup' for short or a pre-marriage contract, is an agreement entered into by a couple shortly before marriage, which is designed to determine what will happen to their property in the event of a divorce. It might, for example, limit the amount of money one spouse can claim against another.

For a long time pre-nuptial contracts were held to be unenforceable in English courts. They were seen to be contrary to public policy in that they sought to remove from the courts the power to determine what order was appropriate following a divorce. In the following decision the courts changed their approach.

KEY CASE ANALYSIS: *Radmacher v Granatino* [2010] UKSC 42

Background

- The husband was French and the wife a wealthy heiress. They signed a pre-nuptial agreement, which said that in the event of a divorce no claim could be brought by either party.
- They separated after eight years.
- The wife sought to rely on the pre-nup to defeat the husband's claim for a share in her wealth.

Principle established

- The majority of their lordships agreed that if the agreement is freely entered into and with a full appreciation of the implications the courts would give effect to it, unless it would not be fair to hold the parties to their agreement.
- In this case the husband was aware of the significance of the document and it would not be unfair to limit his award to the terms set out in the agreement.

This case indicates that the courts will give effect to a pre-nup, but leaves the door open to a number of arguments that a party seeking to persuade the court to depart from a pre-nup can use. First, they may argue that the pre-nup was not entered into freely. Perhaps they were pressurised into signing it. For example, if a spouse on the eve of the marriage said they would not marry unless the other party signed the agreement, it might be felt that these were such pressuring circumstances that the other party was not freely agreeing to the terms.

Second, the party seeking to escape the pre-nup may argue the pre-nup was not entered into with a full appreciation either of the facts (e.g. they were not aware of the wealth of their spouse) or its legal significance. To deal with these first two concerns, good practice is for both spouses to make full disclosure of their finances and ensure independent legal advice is given to each party before the pre-nup is signed.

Third, a party may claim it would not be fair to hold them to the agreement in the light of the event that transpired after the marriage. For example, the agreement may have been entered into on the assumption that both parties would continue their career, but the couple had a disabled child and so one spouse gave up their career.

On-the-spot question

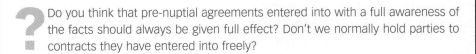

Do you think that pre-nuptial agreements entered into with a full awareness of the facts should always be given full effect? Don't we normally hold parties to contracts they have entered into freely?

One commentator suggested that pre-marriage contracts were the "death knell of marriage" because they allowed people to decide for themselves what they wanted marriage to mean. Is that a fair comment?

THE HOUSE

For many couples their house constitutes their largest asset. Further, when looking at the needs of the parties ensuring there is somewhere to live is a major aspect of needs. These two points mean that accommodation and what should happen to the family home is often one of the most important issues of dispute. Thorpe LJ in *M v B* [1998] has said the court should endeavour if possible to ensure each party is provided with a home.

There are a number of options that might be open to a court in deciding what to do with a house. It may be best to sell the house and divide the proceeds between the couple. However, given the size of many people's mortgages that might not leave sufficient equity to provide much by way of assistance with accommodation.

Another option is to require one spouse to transfer the house (or their share in the house) to the other spouse. That may or may not be in return for capital. So a wife may be required to transfer her share in the house to her husband and in return he will have to pay her £100,000. Typically the spouse with the children will remain in the house, with the other spouse finding accommodation from other assets or even renting.

Another popular order is a "Mesher order", so-called after a case of that name. This order means that the house is put on a trust for certain shares for the couple (it may be 50:50 or some other division). However, the sale is then postponed until a stated event. Typically this is when the children have finished their full-time education or when one spouse has died or remarried. The advantage of these orders is that the spouse who leaves (often the husband) will get to see his money in the end; it is just postponed until the children leave home. It is also sometimes argued that once the children leave home, the wife does not need as big a house and so it is a good time to sell it and allow the wife to downsize.

AGREEMENTS

Commonly couples will reach an agreement about how to divide their property on divorce. The hope is that this will avoid costly legal proceedings. If these agreements are to have effect they need to be presented to court and formalised into a consent order. The court has the power to refuse to agree with the proposed order if it thinks it is manifestly unfair, although that will be very rare. Normally, especially if the parties have been advised by lawyers, the judge will quickly determine that it is appropriate to make an order (known as a consent order) in the terms agreed by the parties.

VARIATION

A court has the power under section 31 to vary or discharge a court order. This can only be done in relation to the orders set out in s 32(2) which include period payments, a lump sum order by instalments and an order for sale of property. There is no power to vary a lump sum order or a property adjustment order. Those orders are often part of a clean break order and are intended to be once and for all.

The court will only vary or discharge an order if it is persuaded that there has been a significant change in the circumstances since the order was made to justify a variation. For example in *Grey v Grey* [2009] the fact the wife had entered a long-term relationship was found to have a clear impact on her needs so as to justify a variation in the sum being paid.

APPEALS

An appeal is normally only allowed where the judge has taken into account irrelevant matters or ignored relevant matters or the result is plainly wrong (*G v G* [1985]. The courts will be very reluctant to allow an appeal especially once the time allowed for appeal has passed.

KEY CASE ANALYSIS: *Barder v Barder* **[1998] AC 20**

Background

- A consent order was made under which the husband agreed to transfer his share in the house to the wife.
- Four weeks later the wife committed suicide and killed the children.
- The time limit for an appeal had passed. He sought leave to appeal out of time.

Principle established

The House of Lords held that in exceptional circumstances leave to appeal out of time could be allowed if:

1 The new events invalidated the fundamental assumption on which the original order would have been made.
2 The new events occurred within a relatively short time of the original order.
3 The application for leave to appeal had been made promptly.
4 Third parties who had acquired property on the basis of the order would not be disadvantaged.

CHILD SUPPORT PAYMENTS

The law on child support has recently changed. In the past child support payments were collected by a government agency, the Child Support Agency. A complex formula was used to calculate how much a non-resident spouse was required to pay the spouse who was caring for the child. In outline, a non-resident parent had to pay 15 per cent of their income for one child; 20 per cent for two children; and 25 per cent for three or more children. However, the scheme proved difficult to operate. Many non-resident parents (primarily fathers) found ways of escaping payment and the formula proved difficult to operate, especially in cases where non-resident parents had fluctuating incomes.

The new system has done away with the Child Support Agency. Instead, couples are encouraged to negotiate agreements themselves. If they need assistance, the couple can be helped by the Child Maintenance Options, which can also help with enforcement. Although it is early days, it is assumed couples are likely to agree lower sums of money than would have been collected under the old scheme. However, the hope is that if couples negotiate these agreements themselves there will be fewer problems enforcing them.

SUMMARY

- The court has a broad discretion to divide the property of the couple on divorce.
- The statute lists factors that are to be taken into account in exercising the discretion.
- In wealthy families the assets will be divided equally between the couple.
- A pre-nuptial agreement will be given effect if entered into appropriately and if it would not be clearly unfair to give it effect.
- The courts will try to make a clean break order so there is no on going liability between the parties.

FURTHER READING

A Barlow and J Smithson, "Is modern marriage a bargain? Exploring perceptions of pre-nuptial agreements in England and Wales" (2012) *Child and Family Law Quarterly* 304 – examines the attitudes of the public towards pre-nups.

E Cooke, "Miller/McFarlane – law in search of discrimination" (2007) *Child and Family Law Quarterly* 98 – examines the role of discrimination in financial orders.

R Deech, "What is a woman worth?" (2009) *Family Law* 1140 – considers whether maintenance should be paid to wives.

P Harris, R George and J Herring, "With this ring I thee wed (terms and conditions apply)" (2011) *Family Law* 367 – criticises the use of pre-nups.

J Herring, "Why financial orders on divorce should be unfair" (2005) 19 *International Journal of Law Policy and the Family* 218 – argues that there is a public interest in how property is divided on divorce.

Chapter 7
Parenthood and parental responsibilities

LEARNING OBJECTIVES

After reading this chapter you should be able to:

- state who is a child's mother in legal terms;
- explain how paternity is allocated;
- understand the concept of parental responsibility.

INTRODUCTION

This chapter will explore who is a child's parent and what rights and responsibilities flow from that. Two major themes will emerge in this chapter. The first is the tension between **biological parenthood** and **social parenthood**.

Key definition: biological parenthood

Biological parenthood refers to those people whose genetic material make up the child. In other words, the father is the man who provided the sperm that led to the creation of the child and the mother is the woman who provided the egg.

Key definition: social parenthood

Social parenthood refers to those who are involved in the day-to-day care of the child, those who spend time with the child and act in a parental way towards them.

In many cases those who are the biological parents will be the same people who are the social parents and there will be no particular difficulty. However, with increasing rates of relationship breakdown it is now common for children to be raised by adults who are not their biological parents. Similarly with the use of assisted reproductive techniques the social parent may not be the biological parent. In such cases the law must decide who is going to be the parent in the eyes of the law: the social parent or the biological parent?

The second (and related) issue is how far the law on parenthood should match what some people regard as "the natural" approach of a child having one mother and one father. This assumption is challenged if we accept that the law should recognise social parenthood, rather than biological parenthood. It is a challenge, in particular, with same-sex parents raising children. To many commentators we need to move beyond the traditional model and be happy to accept a child can have, say, two mothers. To others it is important that the law sticks with the traditional model to reflect the "natural" state of affairs.

In response to both of these issues the courts have developed a somewhat nuanced response by distinguishing parenthood from parental responsibility. Parenthood is the determining of who is the mother and who is the father of the child. Parental responsibility refers to the rights and responsibilities that a parent has. This enables the law to say that although someone is a parent they do not have the rights and responsibilities of being a parent. And similarly to say that although someone is not a parent they do have the rights and responsibilities attached to parenthood.

REAL WORLD

In 2012 there were 729,674 live births in England and Wales. In 2012 the total fertility rate (average number of children per woman) was 1.94. The average age of mothers was 29.8.

WHO IS THE MOTHER OF THE CHILD?

In all cases the woman who gives birth to the child is her mother. This is true even if the mother has become pregnant using a donated egg (and so is not genetically related to the child) and even if the arrangement is a surrogacy arrangement and the woman who gives birth is not expected to care for the child.

> ## Key definition: surrogacy arrangement
>
> In a surrogacy arrangement a couple seeking to have a child (the commissioning couple) agree with a woman (the surrogate mother) to carry a child for them. Sometimes the commissioning couple provide some, or all, of the genetic material. Sometimes the commissioning couple provide none. The surrogacy agreement typically states that after birth the surrogate mother will hand over the child to the commissioning couple and they will raise the child. Normally it is understood that the surrogate mother will play no further role in the child's life. Under English law the surrogate mother cannot be paid (although she can receive compensation for expenses), although in other jurisdictions payment is permitted.

WHO IS THE FATHER OF THE CHILD?

The starting point is that the biological father is the father of the child. That is, the man whose sperm led to the creation of the child is the father. However, the legal position is more complex than that. It relies on various presumptions and also on statutory provisions.

Presumptions of fatherhood

The law will presume that a man is the father of a child in the following situations:

- He is married to the mother at the time of the birth (this is known as the "pater est" presumption).
- He is named on the child's birth certificate as the father.
- The facts imply that he was the biological father (e.g. he was living with the mother at the time of the conception).

It is important to appreciate that these are rebuttable presumptions. They can be rebutted if DNA tests are carried out and they show that in fact the man is not the father of the child. So, for example, if a woman gives birth it will be presumed that her husband is the child's father. If, however, the husband suspects his wife was having an affair, he can seek DNA tests and if they were to show he was not the biological father of the child, the presumption would be rebutted and he would cease to be the father.

If a man is seeking to challenge a presumption (be that he is arguing he should not be presumed to be the father or is seeking to show he is the father), DNA tests can be carried out if the mother agrees. If she does not the man would need a court order seeking tests. As long as there is a good reason for doing the tests then the court is likely to order them unless it could be shown that the tests will cause serious harm to the child (*J v C* [2006]). An application should be brought under the Family Law Act 1969.

Key definition: parentage tests

Family Law Act 1969, s 20(1) states that:

(1) In any civil proceedings in which the parentage of any person falls to be determined, the court may, either of its own motion or on an application by any party to the proceedings, give a direction–

    (a) for the use of scientific tests to ascertain whether such tests show that a party to the proceedings is or is not the father or mother of that person; and

    (b) for the taking, within a period specified in the direction, of bodily samples from all or any of the following, namely, that person, any party who is alleged to be the father or mother of that person and any other party to the proceedings;

    and the court may at any time revoke or vary a direction previously given by it under this subsection.

KEY CASE ANALYSIS: *Re H and A* [2002] EWCA Civ 383

Background

- A man sought parental responsibility and contact with twins who were living with their mother and her husband. The man claimed that he was the father of the children as he had had an extra-marital affair with the mother.
- The mother insisted that her husband was the father of the child.
- The man sought DNA tests to establish whether he was the father.
- The judge refused because the tests could have a negative impact on the family unit.

Principle established

- The court ordered a rehearing.
- There were two key principles that governed these cases: the interests of justice are generally best served by ascertaining the truth and the court should make decisions based on facts and not rely on presumptions.
- These principles needed to be given weight at the rehearing in deciding whether or not to order tests.

KEY CASE ANALYSIS: *Re T (Paternity: Ordering Blood Tests)* [2001] 2 FLR 1190

Background

- The applicant believed he was the father of a child born to his friend's wife. He wanted tests to be done to prove his paternity.
- The mother and her husband objected.

Principle established

- Bodey J emphasised that children had a right under Article 8 to know their genetic origins.
- Even if the DNA test would interfere in the Article 8 rights to respect for their private and family life any interference was justified on the basis that it was necessary to protect the rights of the child.
- In this case it was relevant that there were rumours about the child's paternity and the child was likely to find out about the suspicions at some point anyway. In that case it was better that the truth was known now.

THE HUMAN FERTILISATION AND EMBRYOLOGY ACTS OF 1990 AND 2008

This legislation (the 2008 Act substantially amended the 1990 Act) governs assisted reproductive treatments in the UK. Most relevant for this chapter is that it makes provision for the allocation of parenthood in cases of assisted reproduction. The starting point even in a case of assisted reproduction is that a father is the man whose sperm is used to produce the child. Unless there is a statutory provision that applies otherwise then this is the rule to follow (even if it produces an odd result) as the following case shows:

KEY CASE ANALYSIS: *A v Leeds Teaching Hospital NHS Trust* **[2004] 3 FCR 324**

Background

- Mr and Mrs A were patients at a clinic for fertility treatment.
- In error, the sperm of Mr B, rather than Mr A, was used to fertilise some of Mrs A's eggs.
- The resulting child was placed in Mrs A and twins were born.

Principle established

- Mr B was the father of the child.
- None of the provisions on fatherhood could be relied upon by Mr A or Mr B and so the basic rule was that the genetic father was the father. This was true even though the couples had agreed that Mr and Mrs A were going to raise the child and Mr B was to play no role in the child's life.
- The court suggested that Mr and Mrs A could adopt the child.

Where donated sperm is used at a licensed clinic

If a woman receives assisted reproductive treatment at a licensed clinic then her husband will be the father of the child born, unless he did not consent to her receiving the treatment. This is true even if donated sperm has been used. In such a case the sperm donor will not be the father (s 41). In section 35 there is a similar provision dealing with a woman's female spouse or civil partner. She will be treated as the parent of the child.

The same is true if the "agreed parenthood conditions" are met. If so, a woman's unmarried partner will be the father, or (if female) the "other parent" of the child.

Key definition: the agreed parenthood conditions

Section 37 of the Human Fertilisation and Embryology Act 2008 set these out in relation to a male partner. There is a similarly worded provision for a female partner:

> The agreed fatherhood conditions referred to in section 36(b) are met in relation to a man ("M") in relation to treatment provided to W under a licence if, but only if,–
>
> (a) M has given the person responsible a notice stating that he consents to being treated as the father of any child resulting from treatment provided to W under the licence,
>
> (b) W has given the person responsible a notice stating that she consents to M being so treated,
>
> (c) neither M nor W has, since giving notice under paragraph (a) or (b), given the person responsible notice of the withdrawal of M's or W's consent to M being so treated,
>
> (d) W has not, since the giving of the notice under paragraph (b), given the person responsible–
>
> (i) a further notice under that paragraph stating that she consents to another man being treated as the father of any resulting child, or
>
> (ii) a notice under s 44(1)(b) stating that she consents to a woman being treated as a parent of any resulting child, and
>
> (e) W and M are not within prohibited degrees of relationship in relation to each other.

In short the agreed parenthood provisions mean that if a woman wants someone to be regarded as the parent of her child and they are willing to take on that role, the law will recognise them as a parent in most cases. It is important to emphasise, however, the limited nature of this provision. First, it only applies in cases where treatment is offered in a licensed clinic. It does not apply to cases of "DIY insemination" (e.g. where a woman uses a friend's sperm and inseminates herself with it). Second, the consent of the person to be recognised as a parent is essential. You cannot go along to a clinic and simply name Ryan Gosling as the person you want to be the father of your child!

On-the-spot question

? Notice that if a woman wishes a female partner to be recognised as the parent the partner is not officially known as a mother. She will be called the "other parent". That way the legislation ensures that a child will not have two mothers in the eyes of the law. Is there any justification for that? Or is it, as some have suggested, a reluctance by the courts to fully recognise same-sex relationships?

The position of the sperm/egg donor

If a woman donates an egg or a man donates sperm to be used by others in reproductive treatment then they will not be treated as the parent of the child. However, under the 2008 Act a child born using assisted reproductive treatment has a right, once they are eighteen, to find out who their sperm donor father is. This, it is said, protects the child's right to know his or her genetic parentage. Note, however, that a child has no right to be told that they were born using assisted reproduction. It may well be, therefore, that this right is of less significance in practice than appears at first sight.

FIERCE DEBATE

The right of children to know the identity of their sperm donor fathers has generated debate. It has led to a severe drop in the number of men willing to donate sperm. Indeed sperm has had to be imported from overseas to meet the demand. As already mentioned, some have claimed that the right means little in practice as children have no right to be informed that they were born using donated sperm. Also, children born outside the context of assisted reproduction have no way of finding out who their genetic father was. Against these points is the strong claim made on behalf of children that they have a right to know their genetic origins. Children born using donated sperm claim to be seriously harmed if they cannot find out who their biological father was. There may also be medical reasons why they need to know their parentage. That said it would be possible for medical information about a donor to be provided without disclosing their identity.

Disputes over frozen embryos

What should happen if a couple have an embryo frozen and then stored, but then separate and cannot agree what should happen to it?

KEY CASE ANALYSIS: *Evans v Amicus Health Ltd* [2004] 1 FLR 67

Background

- Ms Evans and Mr Johnson had sought IVF treatment as Ms Evans was undergoing cancer treatment that would render her infertile.
- Some embryos were produced using Ms Evans's eggs and Mr Johnson's sperm.
- The couple later separated and Mr Johnson sought the destruction of the embryos, while Ms Evans wanted to use the embryos to become pregnant.
- She could no longer produce any eggs and this was her only chance of producing a child that was "hers".

Principle established

- The Human Fertilisation and Embryology Act was clear that the embryos could only be stored with the consent of both parties.
- As Mr Johnson no longer consented, the embryos could not lawfully be retained.
- The case went to the European Court of Human Rights. There was a clash of rights in this case both falling under Article 8 of the European Convention: Mr Johnson had the right not to be a parent without his consent and Ms Evans had the right to be a parent, using her genetic material.
- These rights were equally balanced and so the legislation could not be challenged in human rights grounds.

FIERCE DEBATE

Was the Evans decision correct? To some while there was a clash of rights: the clash not to be a parent and the right to be a parent; the court should have found the right to be a parent of greater weight. That is because if a child was born, it might be slightly awkward for Mr Johnson, but it would not really impact on his life (Ms Evans had offered to guarantee she would not seek child support). However, if Ms Evans could not use the embryos she was going to have one of the great goals of her life (to have a child of her own) destroyed. The impact on her of the decision was far greater than it would have been on Mr Johnson if the embryos had been used.
On the other hand it might be argued that the decision reflects gender equality. A woman cannot be forced to be a mother against her will, nor should a father.

SURROGACY

We have already mentioned the practice of **surrogacy**. This is where a woman carries a child for a couple, with the plan being she will hand the child over at birth. The legal position is that at birth the woman who gives birth is the mother. The father will be the man whose genetic material produced the child (unless donor sperm was used through a licensed clinic). If the surrogacy "works" and the child is handed over, the couple can apply for a parental order under s 54 of the Human Fertilisation and Embryology Act 2008, which will make them the parents of the child. However, the grounds for making a parenting order are strict (see below). Couples who cannot apply for such an order can seek to adopt the child.

Key definition: parental order

Who can apply for a parental order is outlined under section 54 of the Human Fertilisation and Embryology Act 1990 as follows:

2   The applicants must be–

   (a)   married,

   (b)   civil partners of each other, or

   (c)   two persons who are living as partners in an enduring family relationship and are not within prohibited degrees of relationship in relation to each other.

3   Except in a case falling within subsection (11), the applicants must apply for the order during the period of 6 months beginning with the day on which the child is born.

4   At the time of the application and the making of the order–

   (a)   the child's home must be with the applicants, and

   (b)   either or both of the applicants must be domiciled in the United Kingdom or in the Channel Islands or the Isle of Man.

5   At the time of the making of the order both the applicants must have attained the age of 18.

6   The court must be satisfied that both–

   (a)   the woman who carried the child, and

   (b)   any other person who is a parent of the child but is not one of the applicants (including any man who is the father by virtue of section 35 or 36 or any woman who is a parent by virtue of section 42 or 43), have freely, and with full understanding of what is involved, agreed unconditionally to the making of the order.

7   Subsection (6) does not require the agreement of a person who cannot be found or is incapable of giving agreement; and the agreement of the woman who carried the child is ineffective for the purpose of that subsection if given by her less than six weeks after the child's birth.

8   The court must be satisfied that no money or other benefit (other than for expenses reasonably incurred) has been given or received by either of the applicants for or in consideration of–

(a)   The making of the order,

(b)   any agreement required by subsection (6),

(c)   the handing over of the child to the applicants, or

(d)   the making of arrangements with a view to the making of the order, unless authorised by the court.

KEY CASE ANALYSIS: *Re G (Surrogacy)* [2007] EWHC 2814

Background

- An English surrogate mother agreed to give birth and pass the child on to a married couple in Turkey.
- The child was produced using the egg of the surrogate mother and the Turkish husband's sperm.
- The surrogate mother was married but no longer lived with her husband.
- The Turkish couple came to collect the child and there was some difficulty in determining how to deal with the situation.

Principle established

- As the husband had not given his consent it was presumed that he was the father.
- However, in this case it was clear the presumption could be rebutted and the Turkish husband was the biological father. An order under section 30, a parental order, could not be made because the Turkish couple were not resident in the UK.

- The best order was that the Turkish couple adopt the child.
- Under section 84 of the Adoption and Children Act 2002 they could be given parental responsibility as potential adopters.

If payments are made to the surrogate mother then a parental order can only be made if the payments are limited to reasonable expenses or if in excess of that they are authorised by the courts. In fact the courts have become increasingly generous in authorising payments. In *Re X and Y (Parental Orders: Retrospective Authorisation of Payments)* [2011] £27,000 payment was authorised. It was held that the payments were not disproportionate to the expenses and it was in the children's interests to be brought by the commissioning parents in an officially recognised way. The parental order was therefore made.

Sometimes the surrogacy does not work and the surrogate mother refuses to hand over the child. In that case the matter is likely to go to court and the court will determine what order is in the best interests of the child (*Re P (Surrogacy: Residence)* [2008]). The courts normally allow the child to remain with her mother, unless there is evidence she is unsuitable. This reflects the clear position in English law that a surrogacy contract is not enforceable.

On-the-spot question

? Should surrogacy contracts be enforceable? To some surrogacy contracts should be enforceable, like any other contract (although note that the normal remedy for breach of contract is that damages are paid, rather than that the other party must perform the contract). To others the surrogate mother has invested so much more of herself in the child (through the pregnancy) that she has a stronger claim to him or her than the commissioning mother, who may only have paid money.

PARENTAL RESPONSIBILITY

As mentioned in the introduction, there is an important distinction between being a parent and having parental responsibility. Parental responsibility is the legal term used to describe the rights and responsibilities that a parent has in connection with a child.

Who gets parental responsibility

All mothers automatically get parental responsibility. For fathers the position is more complicated. The following fathers have parental responsibility:

- a father married to the mother;
- a father registered on the birth certificate (section 4 Children Act 1989);
- a father who has entered into a parental responsibility agreement with the mother;
- a father who has obtained a parental responsibility order from the court;
- a father who has obtained a residence order from the court;
- a father who has adopted his child;
- a step parent or a female non-biological parent in a civil partnership or marriage with the mother can acquire parental responsibility in these ways too.

If a father applies for a parental responsibility order from the court, it will assess whether giving him an order will promote the child's welfare.

Others can only acquire parental responsibility by applying for and obtaining a residence order in respect of the child. As the following cases indicate, it is rare that a father will not obtain parental responsibility.

KEY CASE ANALYSIS: *Re S (Parental Responsibility)* [1995] 2 FLR 648

Background

- An unmarried couple had a child together.
- The couple separated when a father was convicted of possessing paedophilic literature.
- The father applied for parental responsibility.

Principle established

- Parental responsibility involved an acknowledgement that the father was committed to the child. It would send the message to the father that he cared for the child and was attached to her.
- The father was not allowed contact with the child and so the extent to which he could exercise parental responsibility was limited. He was warned that if he misused it it would be removed.

KEY CASE ANALYSIS: *Re M (A Child) (Parental Responsibility: Welfare: Status)* [2013] EWCA Civ 969

Background

- M was born in 2002. His father was on the birth certificate but under the law at that time this was insufficient to give him parental responsibility.
- He and the mother raised the child together until 2007.
- After the separation the father had a significant relationship with M. In 2008 he removed M from school without warning the mother and he returned M to school the following day.
- The mother at that point sought a residence order and no contact order. The father sought parental responsibility and contact.
- A psychologist gave evidence that M did not want his father to know his home or school address but was happy to have supervised contact.

Principle established

- The judge accepted the father was committed to M and they were attached. However the judge was concerned that the father would use parental responsibility as a way of exercising control over M and M's mother.
- It was held that it would be rare not to order parental responsibility if a father sought it. However, that did not mean there was a presumption in favour of granting parental responsibility.
- If the judge was concerned about misuse of parental responsibility it was necessary to consider the extent and nature of the potential misuse. These had to be sufficient to decline parental responsibility.
- It should be recalled that restrictions on the use of parental responsibility could be invoked to restrict misuse. The Court of Appeal upheld the order because it could not be said that the judge had made an error of law.
- The judge had taken into account the vulnerability of the mother and the wishes of the child and the fears of misuse in declining parental responsibility and that was appropriate.

FIERCE DEBATE

Is the fact that mothers automatically get parental responsibility but fathers do not an example of family law being sexist? Some commentators certainly think so. It is true that some fathers lack commitment and do not deserve parental responsibility, but that is true of some mothers too. Others argue that if parental responsibility demonstrates commitment to the child, we can presume that all mothers are committed and it is not unreasonable to presume that a man who is not married to the mother, has not had himself listed as the father on the birth certificate, and has not taken steps to obtain parental responsibility is not committed.

KEY CASE ANALYSIS: *B v UK* [2000] 1 FLR 1

Background

- An unmarried father did not have parental responsibility automatically for his child under UK law.
- He claimed that the UK law breached ECHR Article 8 and was discriminatory under Article 14.

Principle established

- The relationship between an unmarried father and his children varies from ignorance and indifference to a close stable relationship.
- This difference provided an objective and reasonable justification for treating married and unmarried fathers differently in relation to the automatic acquisition of parental responsibility.

What is parental responsibility?

Key definition: parental repsonsibility

The Children Act 1989 s 3(1) states that: "'Parental responsibility' means all the rights, duties, powers, responsibilities and authority, which by law a parent of a child has in relation to the child and his property".

The concept of parental responsibility is used to refer to the legal rights and responsibilities that attach to parents. It is interesting that the statute calls the concept parental responsibility (rather than parental rights). This was to send the message that parents should understand their role as being about responsibilities rather than rights.

KEY CASE ANALYSIS: *Re B (A Minor) (Wardship: Medical Treatment)* [1990] 3 All ER 927

Background

- A child was born with Down's syndrome.
- She had an intestinal blockage and needed a life-saving operating to remove it.
- The parents did not think the child should live and refused to consent to the operation.

Principle established

- The judge approved the procedure.
- The parents did not have the right to decide whether the child would live or die.
- The judge would decide whether the operation was in the child's interests and it clearly was.
- No parent would be forced to look after this child. If they did not want to look after the child there were many would-be adoptive parents who would do so.

Note also that the statute has clearly decided not to try and actually state what these rights are. It is generally agreed that it includes issues such as the following:

- medical treatment
- choosing names
- education
- consent to adoption
- housing of the child
- diet.

However, there are so many different situations in which a parent may have to make a decision about a child that it is probably sensible that the legalisation does not produce a list.

KEY CASE ANALYSIS: *M v M (Parental Responsibility)* [1999] 2 FLR 737

Background

- An unmarried father had learning difficulties and had been involved in a motorcycle accident.
- He wanted to acquire parental responsibility for his child.

Principle established

- His mental capacity meant that he could not make decisions on behalf of the child.
- Even though he was committed to the child and loved him, he should not be given parental responsibility.

Consultation

Key definition: independent parental responsibility principle

The Children Act section 2(7) states:

> Where more than one person has parental responsibility for a child, each of them may act alone and without the other (or others) in meeting that responsibility; but nothing in this Part shall be taken to affect the operation of any enactment that requires the consent of more than one person in a matter affecting the child.

This provision indicates that if someone has parental responsibility for a child they can make decisions about the child without consulting the other parent. At one level this makes sense. If a parent is looking after a child and decides to give the child an ice cream, it would be unrealistic to expect the parent to phone up the other parent to ensure she is happy with that. However, the issue is less straightforward when the matter to be decided is a really important one.

> ### KEY CASE ANALYSIS: *Re J (Specific Issue Orders: Child's Religious Upbringing and Circumcision)* [2000] 1 FLR 571
>
> ### Background
>
> - A Muslim father and Christian mother had separated.
> - Their child lived with the mother, but had contact with the father.
> - There arose disputes over whether the child should be circumcised in line with Muslim tradition and what religion the child should have.
>
> ### Principle established
>
> - Over important issues parents should consult with each other.
> - The father could not rely on s 2(7) to justify arranging a circumcision of the child, without the agreement of the mother.
> - As the parents could not agree on circumcision the court needed to resolve the dispute and decided that the circumcision was not in the interests of the child.
> - In relation to the religious dispute the mother would be permitted to discuss Christianity when the child was with her and the father could discuss Islam. It would not be appropriate to determine that the child was Muslim or Christian. The child could when older choose which religion, if any, to adopt.

SUMMARY

- A mother is the woman who gives birth to the child.
- The man is the genetic father normally, but there are provisions dealing with sperm donation and assisted reproduction, which will displace this.
- The law will presume a man is the father in certain cases, such as where he is married to the mother.
- Parental responsibility is given to some fathers, but all mothers.

FURTHER READING

A Bainham, "Is legitimacy legitimate?" (2009) *Family Law* 673 – examines the concept of legitimacy.

A Bainham, "Is anything now left of parental rights?" in R Probert, S Gilmore and J Herring, *Responsible Parents and Parental Responsibility* (Hart, 2009) – considers whether parents have rights.

A Diduck, "'If only we can find the appropriate terms to use the issue will be solved': Law, identity and parenthood" (2007) *Child And Family Law Quarterly* 458 – considers the legal response to same-sex parents.

J Fortin, "Children's rights to know their origins: Too far, too fast" (2009) *Child and Family Law Quarterly* 336 – examines whether children have a right to know their origins.

K Horsey, "Challenging presumptions: Legal parenthood and surrogacy arrangements" (2010) *Child and Family Law Quarterly* 499 – a discussion of the law on surrogacy.

J Wallbank, "'Bodies in the shadows': Joint birth registration, parental responsibility and social class" (2009) *Child and Family Law Quarterly* 267 – a critical look at the law on parental responsibility and proposed reforms.

Chapter 8
Disputes over children

LEARNING OBJECTIVES

After reading this chapter you should be able to:

- learn how a court resolves disputes over children;
- understand the nature and status of children's rights;
- explain the meaning of the welfare principle.

INTRODUCTION

When a couple separate there are often disputes over children. This chapter considers how these are resolved by the courts. It looks at the factors that are taken into account and how they are weighed in deciding what order would best promote the welfare of the child. However, the chapter starts with a consideration of whether or not children have rights.

CHILDREN'S RIGHTS

Do children have rights? Before looking at the law on this question, it is worth thinking about it as a matter of theoretical issue. Whether children have rights is a controversial question in both morality and law. Some commentators argue that children simply lack the maturity to have rights. They are too young to make decisions for themselves and so they cannot access rights until they are old enough. However, that view can be challenged in two ways.

First, some rights may not be dependent on having maturity. For example, do babies not have a right to life? So we might claim that children have some of the rights of adults: those that do not depend on the ability to make a decision.

Second, is it right that all children lack capacity to make decisions? Some children are particularly mature for their age. Indeed they may be as mature as many adults. In that case should we deny them rights? Indeed is it not ageist to say a child cannot have rights simply based on their age?

To some extent the law bypasses some of the more theoretical aspects of the debates. A child's rights are protected in many ways. So, for example, a child is protected by the law on murder, just like anyone else. Further a child is entitled to the rights under the European Convention on Human Rights. However, the law likewise restricts other rights. A child cannot marry until they are 16 and cannot vote until they are 18; similarly there are restrictions on when a child can buy alcohol. These regulations tend to be accepted without question. Clearly one benefit of them is that they are workable. The publican can refuse to serve a fourteen-year-old child, without having to do an on-the-spot analysis of the child's maturity.

The following case is often quoted as a landmark case for recognising that children have rights.

KEY CASE ANALYSIS: *Gillick v West Norfolk and Wisbech Health Authority* [1986] AC 112 (HL)

Background

- The Department of Health had issued a circular telling doctors it was lawful for them to prescribe contraception to girls under 16.
- Doctors did not need the consent of the girls' parents to do this.
- Mrs Gillick had five daughters and was opposed to contraception on religious grounds. She sought a declaration the circular was illegal.

Principle established

- The circular was lawful.
- As long as the doctor was persuaded that the child was sufficiently competent to understand the issues involved and that the treatment was in her best interests the doctor could provide contraceptive treatment.
- There was no need to obtain the consent of the girls' parents.

The principle in that case was confirmed in *R (Axon) v Secretary of State for Health* [2006] where a similar issue arose, this time on whether a doctor could discuss and arrange an abortion for a girl under 16 without her parents' consent. Silber J confirmed the doctor could. The mother had relied upon the Human Rights Act 1998 to claim a parent had a right to be consulted but Silber J argued that once a child was sufficiently mature to make a decision for herself the parents lost their right to make decisions for their children.

The *Gillick* decision, confirmed in *Axon*, states that if a child is competent the child can consent to treatment. But somewhat surprisingly the courts have decided it does not follow if a child is competent she can effectively refuse treatment.

KEY CASE ANALYSIS: *Re R (A Minor)(Wardship: Medical Treatment)* [1992] Fam 11 (CA)

Background

- R was a fifteen-year-old girl in an adolescent psychiatric unit. She refused to consent to psychiatric treatment.
- Her parents consented to it.
- Her capacity was fluctuating.

Principle established

Even if a child is *Gillick* competent the doctor could provide medical treatment if consent was provided by a parent with parental responsibility.

On-the-spot question

 Can you think of any justification for why a child who has capacity to make the decision should have their view given legal weight if it is a consent but not a refusal?

Lord Donnaldson in *Re W* [2012] explains the position taken in this way. A doctor who is providing medical treatment is committing a legal wrong against the child and needs a legal "flak jacket" to make sure the treatment is lawful. The flak jacket can come from one of three sources:

- a child who has sufficient maturity to understand the issue;
- a parent with parental responsibility for a child; or
- a court order.

So the child, if competent, can provide the "flak jacket" but if she does not want to the parent or court can provide the flak jacket instead.

CHILDREN IN COURT

One of the difficulties facing those who believe children should have legal rights is the question of how they are to be enforced. If we say that children have rights, but do not give children the ability to enforce those rights then there is a problem. Indeed there is a real danger that if children cannot go to court their rights will be enforced by adults and only when adults want to enforce them.

The Children Act 1989 allows children to bring proceedings. However, any fear that this may lead to children seeking an order from a court that their parents take them to Disney Land would be ill founded. Before a child can bring proceedings they need the leave of the court. In *Re SC* the court heard an application by a girl who wanted to leave her parents and move in with her best friend. The court refused to grant leave because the issue was seen as trivial. However, if the court is convinced there is a serious issue then a child may be allowed to be involved.

KEY CASE ANALYSIS: *Mabon v Mabon* [2005] EWCA Civ 634

Background

- The parents of three boys were divorcing and disputed the residence.
- The boys wanted to make sure their views were heard in court and wanted a barrister to represent them.

Principle established

- The court agreed that mature articulate children had the right to be involved in cases involving them.
- They had rights protected by the ECHR to freedom of expression and respect for the family life.
- The appointment of a guardian, who would advise the court on what he or she thought best for a child, was not necessarily enough to ensure the views of the child were heard.

REAL WORLD

Despite the decision in *Mabon* the difficulties in funding have meant it is rare that there is money available to ensure that the children receive independent representation.

THE WELFARE PRINCIPLE

Key definition: the welfare principle

The Children Act 1989, section 1 defines the welfare principle as follows:

(1)   When a court determines any question with respect to–

(a)   the upbringing of a child; or

(b)   the administration of a child's property or the application of any income arising from it, the child's welfare shall be the court's paramount consideration.

(2)   In any proceedings in which any question with respect to the upbringing of a child arises, the court shall have regard to the general principle that any delay in determining the question is likely to prejudice the welfare of the child.

(3)   In the circumstances mentioned in subsection (4), a court shall have regard in particular to–

(a)   the ascertainable wishes and feelings of the child concerned (considered in the light of his age and understanding);

(b)   his physical, emotional and educational needs;

(c)   the likely effect on him of any change in his circumstances;

(d)   his age, sex, background and any characteristics of his which the court considers relevant;

(e)   any harm which he has suffered or is at risk of suffering;

(f)   how capable each of his parents, and any other person in relation to whom the court considers the question to be relevant, is of meeting his needs;

(g)   the range of powers available to the court under this Act in the proceedings in question.

Section 1 of the Children Act 1989, just quoted, states that the courts, when determining what order to make in relation to an application under the Act, should put the welfare of the child as the paramount consideration. This means that the court should not place weight on what would be best for the parents or other children, but rather focus on the child at the centre of the case. Indeed even ideas of what is fair should not be used to displace an assessment of what is in the interests of the child.

In section 1(3), quoted above, there is a list of factors that the court should take into account in each case. They are not ranked but rather are to be seen as a checklist for the court to ensure that in its welfare assessment all the relevant matters are considered.

THE NO ORDER PRINCIPLE

Key definition: no order principle

The Children Act 1989, s 1(5) states:

> Where a court is considering whether or not to make one or more orders under this Act with respect to a child, it shall not make the order or any of the orders unless it considers that doing so would be better for the child than making no order at all.

This provision was interpreted by some to mean there is a presumption against making an order. However in *Re G (Children)(Residence Order: No Order Principle)* [2006] Ward LJ held that there was no presumption created by s 1(5). Rather the court simply had to consider whether or not making an order would be better than making no order at all.

The limits of the welfare principle

It is easy to exaggerate the significance of the welfare principle. The welfare principle is not saying that parents must always put the interests of their children above their own. Nor is it saying that public authorities need always put the interests of children first. It is addressed specifically to courts when hearing cases that involve a dispute between parents and requires them to then put the interests of children first. The following case demonstrates that well.

KEY CASE ANALYSIS: *Local Authority v SB, AB and MB* **[2010] EWHC 1744 (Fam)**

Background

- A boy aged 6 had a rare brain disease. A medical report by the medical expert recommended a particular surgery.
- His parents refused to consent. The hospital was happy to comply with the parents' wishes.
- The local authority sought a court order to order the surgery to go ahead.

Principle established

- Neither the parents nor the hospital had sought to bring the matter to the court.
- The local authority had no basis for intervention, unless they were seeking to bring care proceedings, which they were not.

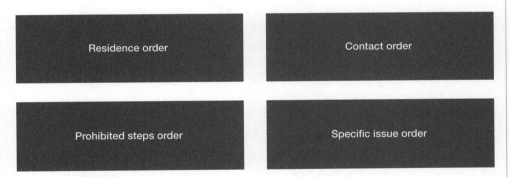

Figure 8.1 Section 8 orders

- **Residence order**: this determines where the child should live.
- **Contact order**: this determines whether a child should visit or have communication with someone.
- A **prohibited steps order**: this stops someone exercising parental responsibility in a particular way (e.g. it prevents a parent taking a child out of the country or stops a parent feeding a child a particular kind of food).
- **Specific steps order**: this determines an issue of dispute over parental responsibility (e.g. over where a child should go to school or whether a child should receive a particular medical treatment.

CHILDREN AND FAMILIES ACT 2014

When the Children and Families Act 2014 comes into force, contact and residence orders will be replaced with child arrangement orders

---

Key definition: child arrangement order

The Children and Families Act 2014, section 12 states:

> "[C]hild arrangements order" means an order regulating arrangements relating to any of the following–
> (a) with whom a child is to live, spend time or otherwise have contact, and
> (b) when a child is to live, spend time or otherwise have contact with any person.

This is just really a change of name. The order will determine with whom the child will live and how much contact the child will have with either parent. The reason behind the change in terminology is an attempt to get away from the idea that there is a "resident parent", with whom the child lives primarily and is therefore the most important parent.

Restrictions on section 8 orders

There are a number of restrictions on when section 9 orders can be made, as shown in Table 8.1 below.

Table 8.1 Restrictions on section 8 orders

Restriction	Section of Children Act 1989
Only a residence order can be made in relation to a child in local authority care	9(1)
Local authority cannot apply for a residence or contact order	9(2)
Local authority foster parent cannot apply for leave to apply for section order in relation to foster child without consent of local authority	9(3)
SIO and PSO cannot be used to achieve what a residence or contact order can achieve	9(5)
Unless there are exceptional circumstances a contact order, SIO, or PSO cannot last beyond the child's sixteenth birthday	9(6)
Once the child is 16 unless there are exceptional circumstances a section 8 order cannot be made	9(7)

REAL WORLD

Family law does much to encourage parents to resolve disputes between themselves, without bringing the matter to court. Baroness Hale in *Holmes-Moorhouse v LB of Richmond upon Thames* [2009] explains why:

> [T]he parents know their own children better than anyone. They also know their own circumstances, what will suit them best, what resources are available and what they can afford. Agreed solutions tend to work much better and last much longer than solutions imposed by a court after contested proceedings. The contest is likely to entrench opposing viewpoints and inflame parental conflict. Conflict is well known to be bad for children.

What she does not mention is the cost to the legal aid budget of these cases. That has become the major influencing feature because legal aid is now severely restricted in disputes over children. Parents are strongly encouraged to resolve disputes themselves.

NATURAL PARENT PRESUMPTION

One issue that has troubled the courts over the years is whether, in determining what is in the welfare of a child, there is a presumption that the child should be raised by his or her biological parents.

KEY CASE ANALYSIS: *Re G (Children)(Residence: Same-Sex Partner)* [2006] UKHL 42

Background

- CG and CW were a lesbian couple who had two daughters. CG was the girl's genetic and gestational mother. The couple raised the children equally.
- CW applied for contact and shared residence when the relationship broke down. Initially a shared residence arrangement was agreed.
- CG moved to Cornwall and the arrangement broke down.

- The judge, affirmed on appeal, gave residence to CW as she was more committed to there being shared care.

Principle established

- The children's primary home should be with CG the biological mother.
- The welfare of the child was the deciding test for where the child should live.
- The factors were finely balanced between the two women, but the fact CG was the "natural mother" had not been given weight by the lower courts.

Baroness Hale said:

The fact that CG is the natural mother of these children in every sense of that term, while raising no presumption in her favour, is undoubtedly an important and significant factor in determining what will be best for them now and in the future.

Lord Nichols, agreeing said:

In reaching its decision the court should always have in mind that in the ordinary way the rearing of a child by his or her biological parent can be expected to be in the child's best interests, both in the short term and also, importantly, in the longer term. I decry any tendency to diminish the significance of this factor. A child should not be removed from the primary care of his or her biological parents without compelling reasons.

But, that case needs to be read alongside the following more recent case.

KEY CASE ANALYSIS: *Re B (A Child)(Residence)* [2009] UKSC 5

Background

- A boy, aged 4, had been raised by his maternal grandparents. His parents had not been able to care for him at birth due to a range of difficulties.
- His parents had separated, but H's father had not resolved many of his difficulties and sought an order that the child live with him.

- The magistrates refused the residence order. They heard evidence that the grandparents were providing excellent care, and although the father could offer "good enough" care for the son, it was below that offered by the grandparents.
- The circuit judge and Court of Appeal supported the father's appeal that insufficient weight had been given to the fact the father was the biological father of the child.

Principle established

- The central factor in all cases involving children was what was in the welfare of the child.
- *Re G* was stating that normally it is best for children to be raised by their natural parents, but that does not mean it is true in every case.
- The judge had to consider the facts of the particular case and what was generally beneficial for children was not particularly helpful in considering what was best for a particular child.
- It was completely wrong to suggest that there is a right for a child to be raised by her natural parents.
- The court focuses on what is in the child's welfare. The order leaving the child with the grandparents was upheld, with regular contact with the father.

It seems then that the natural parent factor is something to be taken into account, but perhaps will only really weigh greatly in a case like *Re G*, where the other factors were very finely balanced.

SHARED RESIDENCE

Key definition: shared residence order

A shared residence order is an order where a child spends roughly equal time with each parent. There is not an exact definition, but once the child is aged 16 or over the time split is closer to equal than 1/3: 2/3.

At one time it was rare for courts to award shared residence. It was thought to be rare for shared residence orders to be suitable because they were unsettling for children and encouraged animosity for the adults. This is no longer a popular attitude.

KEY CASE ANALYSIS: *D v D* [2001] 1 FLR 495

Background

- On the marriage breakdown the children spent a roughly equal amount of time with each parent.
- There was ongoing animosity and the father sought to confirm the arrangement with a shared residence order.
- It was granted and the mother appealed to the Court of Appeal.

Principle established

- It was not necessary to show that there were exceptional circumstances before making a shared residence order (SRO).
- It did not need to be shown there was a clear benefit to the child before an SRO was made.
- The court could make an SRO if doing so would promote the welfare of the child.

More recently in *Re AR (A Child: Relocation)* [2010] Mostyn J suggested that an SRO is "the rule rather than the exception". However, in *T v T* [2010] Black LJ suggested that had gone too far. The position was that a shared residence order could be made where doing so would be in the best interests of the child.

Generally where the parents are on very bad terms an SRO is inappropriate. That is especially where the court fears that the parents will use the child to harm the other parent (*Re K (Share Residence Order)* [2008]. If the parties live a long way apart it may be that an SRO is normally inappropriate. The court will be concerned that travelling long distances regularly will disturb the child and impact on their education.

KEY CASE ANALYSIS: *Re C (A Child)* **[2006] EWCA 235**

Background

- The child got on well with both parents. She was described as being "happy and confident" when living with either parent.
- The parents lived close to each other and the school. The child understood herself as having two homes.

Principle established

The facts of the case were described as a paradigm case for making a shared residence order.

FIERCE DEBATE

Should there be a formal presumption of shared residence? Some have argued in favour of this, arguing that the current law tends to work against the interests of fathers. Others believe that on separation couples often move apart and there is animosity. Requiring a child to spend equal amounts of time with each parent might make the parents feel happier, but will not be good for the child.

CONTACT ORDERS

A contact order can take several forms including the forms shown in Figure 8.2.

Contact orders have become a source of fierce debate in some cases. Fortunately a study found that more than nine in ten parents are able to resolve disputes over contact themselves. However, there are around 10 per cent of couples who apply to court, although even most of those are able to resolve the issue before a full hearing. Cases that require a court order tend, if anything, to make matters worse. Wall J, when president of Family Division once stated:

> The law, which of necessity operates within the discipline of defined orders is, in my judgment, ill-suited to deal with the complex family dynamics inherent in

disputed contact applications. Arrangements for contact stand more prospect of enduring if they are consensual. Wherever possible, contact disputes should be dealt with outside the courtroom.

Despite these comments courts still need to resolve disputes over contact.

The law is relatively easy to state. Contact will be ordered when it is in the welfare of the child to order contact. There have been attempts to persuade the court that it should declare a child has a right of contact with each parent or that there should be a presumption that contact should be ordered. However, the courts have generally been very reluctant to agree to that.

In *Re W (Children)* [2012] MacFarlane LJ explained that the court would note that it was generally good for children to have contact with their parents, but:

> When a court determines any question with respect to the upbringing of a child, the child's welfare must be the court's paramount consideration (CA 1989, s 1(1)).

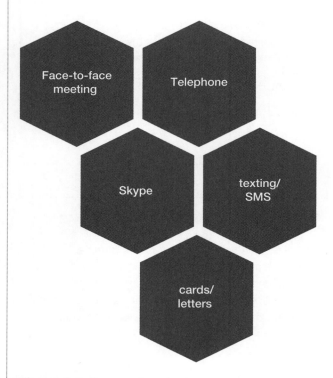

Figure 8.2 Forms of contact

The paramountcy principle in CA 1989, s 1(1), coloured as it is by the requirement of the court to have regard in particular to the aspects of welfare set out in the welfare checklist in s 1(3), is the sole statutory mandate directing the course that a court is to take in determining issues relating to the welfare of a child. Although the case of each child before a court will be unique and will justify careful scrutiny and a bespoke conclusion tailored to meet the particular welfare requirements of that young individual, the courts have nevertheless developed general approaches which indicate the contours of the landscape within which welfare determinations are likely to be taken when there is a dispute between a child's parents.

He then approved Wall J's statement in *Re P (Contact: Supervision)* [1996] as an example of the general approaches he was talking about:

1   Overriding all else, as provided by s 1(1) of the 1989 Act, the welfare of the child is the paramount consideration, and the court is concerned with the interests of the mother and the father only insofar as they bear on the welfare of the child.

2   It is almost always in the interests of a child whose parents are separated that he or she should have contact with the parent with whom the child is not living.

3   The court has power to enforce orders for contact, which it should not hesitate to exercise where it judges that it will overall promote the welfare of the child to do so.

4   Cases do, unhappily and infrequently but occasionally, arise in which a court is compelled to conclude that in existing circumstances an order for immediate direct contact should not be ordered, because so to order would injure the welfare of the child.

5   In cases in which, for whatever reason, direct contact cannot for the time being be ordered, it is ordinarily highly desirable that there should be indirect contact so that the child grows up knowing of the love and interest of the absent parent.

In many cases that actually reach the courts, the resident parent is objecting to contact on the basis that she has suffered domestic abuse in the past and is worried that contact will be used to continue or perpetuate that abuse. The leading case on the issues is the following:

KEY CASE ANALYSIS: *Re L, V, M and H (Contact: Domestic Violence)* [2000] 2 FLR 334

Background

- Four cases were held together by the Court of Appeal.
- In all of them fathers had been violent or threatened violence to the mothers (that had been proved).
- The mothers were fearful and opposed contact.

Principle established

- It would be wrong to say that where there had been domestic violence there was a presumption against ordering contact.
- The courts must, however, take allegations of domestic violence seriously.
- It is a "highly important" factor in contact cases.
- The courts must consider the seriousness of the violence, the risks involved and the impact on the child of contact following domestic violence and weigh that against any benefits of contact.
- The extent of the violence, the effect of the violence on the primary carer and child, and the ability of the offender to recognise his past behaviour and seek to make a change.

When the 2014 Children and Families Act comes into effect, it will insert a new provision into section 1 of the Children Act 1989, which is designed to encourage courts to make contact orders. It requires courts "to presume, unless the contrary is shown, that involvement of that parent in the life of the child concerned will further the child's welfare". This only applies to a parent if "that parent can be involved in the child's life in a way that does not put the child at risk of suffering harm". The court will require evidence to be persuaded that the parental involvement will put the child at risk. The court makes it clear that involvement in the child's welfare can include indirect contact.

FIERCE DEBATE

It remains to be seen whether the 2014 reforms will make much of a change in the law. It is unlikely under the current law that the court would refuse to make a contact order unless there was some evidence that the parent would cause harm to the child. However, the courts may interpret this provision to create a strong presumption in favour of contact.

ENFORCING CONTACT

Even if a court decides to make a contact order there are major problems in enforcing contact. Indeed Baroness Hale in *Re G (Children) (residence: same-sex partner)* [2006] said that the enforcement of contact was "one of the most difficult and contentious challenges in the whole of family law".

The most common scenario is as follows. The court has made an order that a father have contact with his child. The child lives with the mother and she is fearful of the father and refuses to allow contact. The father brings the matter to court.

Normally if a person breaks a court order they are imprisoned for contempt of court. Occasionally the courts have been willing to do this in contact cases. However few people think that is a satisfactory solution to the problem. It is likely to turn the child against the father and having a mother imprisoned is likely to harm the child. Another alternative may be a fine, but again that will not produce a solution to the problem and may just harm the child.

The Government sought to introduce some new solutions in the Children and Adoption Act 2006, which introduced three orders that may help in some cases:

1   Contact activity directions and conditions. This can direct a party to the proceedings to attend a class, counselling, guidance, information and advice about contact or mediation. It may be appropriate, for example, to send the resident parent on a programme to encourage them to understand the benefits of contact for their children. Alternatively it may encourage both parties to attend mediation and see if they can talk through the issues that are making contact difficult.

2   The court can take an unpaid work requirement for the person breaching the order. This might involve some kind of community service.

3   The court can ask a CAFCASS officer to monitor contact. This might be helpful in a case where there is a dispute over who is creating problems with contact orders.

CHANGING NAMES

Perhaps surprisingly, there has been a string of cases on children's names. A typical scenario is this. A child is born to a married couple and given the couple's name. The couple divorce and the child lives with the mother. She remarries and decides to take her new husband's name. She then wishes to change her child's name to her new name so that the child is integrated into the "new family". However, the father objects on the basis that he is being "written out" of the child's life.

A parent is allowed to change the name of a child unless there is a residence order in force in respect of the child, in which case written consent is required (s 13(1)(b) Children Act 1989). In other cases the parent should consult with the other party before changing the name, although there does not seem to be any legal consequence of failing to do so.

The courts have taken the view that changing the name of a child is a serious matter (*Dawson v Wearmouth* [1999]). Generally the case is a matter of the child's welfare, but the courts will require a good reason to allow a change. Stopping a father who poses a risk to a child from finding the child would be a good reason (*Re F (Contact)* [2007]). The courts have also placed weight on the fact the child has got used to the new name and it would be disruptive to return the child to the previous name.

In *Re S (Surname: Using Both Parents' Surname)* [2001] the Court of Appeal made the sensible suggestion that parents be encouraged to give the child a double surname: one chosen by the mother and the other by the father. This seems a sensible solution to these disputes.

RELOCATION CASES

One topic that has attracted considerable debate is cases involving relocation. Typically the scenario is as follows. A couple separate and the child lives with the mother and has regular contact with the mother. The mother wishes to take the children to live in another country. Perhaps she wishes to return to her county of origin or to take up a new job or join a new partner. The father objects to the move because it will severely impact on his contact. This issue has become more common because increasingly people marry internationally and there is more opportunity to move between countries.

The law states that if a parent wishes to remove a child from the jurisdiction they must have the consent of everyone with parental responsibility. If they do not they will commit the crime of kidnap or child abduction. If the resident parent seeks consent and the other parent refuses the matter may then be taken to court either by way of an application of a specific issue order to allow relocation or a prohibited steps order to prevent it. If a residence order is in force an application can be made by applying under section 13.

Subsequent case law has reinforced the point that at the end of the day the guidance in *Payne* is about ensuring that the welfare principle is followed. While it is true that where the courts have been persuaded that the primary carer is making a reasonable decision in seeking to move overseas and that it will be harmful to the child not to allow the move leave will normally be granted, that is not a legal presumption. In *Re H (A Child)* [2007] Thorpe LJ thought that the impact on the caring parent of a refusal to grant leave to move was "often the most important single task that confronts the judge" in these kinds of cases.

KEY CASE ANALYSIS: *Payne v Payne* **[2001] EWCA Civ 1166**

Background

- On separation the daughter lived with the mother. She wished to move to New Zealand.
- The father had regular contact with the daughter.
- The mother sought leave to remove the child from the jurisdiction.

Principle established

- The court should apply the welfare principle.
- It was wrong to suggest (as previous case law had done) that if the proposal was a reasonable one permission to relocate would be given.
- The judge should consider all the factors to assess the welfare. However, if there was a genuine motivation for the move and it was not an attempt to defeat the contact with the other parent, then leave would be likely to be given. That is because an important factor would be the impact on the primary carer of forcing her to remain in the country against her will.

Thorpe LJ set out a four-stage process later cases have followed:

(a) Pose the question: is the mother's application genuine in the sense that it is not motivated by some selfish desire to exclude the father from the child's life. Then ask is the mother's application realistic, by which I mean founded on practical proposals both well researched and investigated? If the application fails either of these tests refusal will inevitably follow.

(b) If however the application passes these tests then there must be a careful appraisal of the father's opposition: is it motivated by genuine concern for the future of the child's welfare or is it driven by some ulterior motive? What would be the extent of the detriment to him and his future relationship with the child were the application granted? To what extent would that be offset by extension of the child's relationships with the maternal family and homeland?

(c) What would be the impact on the mother, either as the single parent or as a new wife, of a refusal of her realistic proposal?

(d) The outcome of the second and third appraisals must then be brought into an overriding review of the child's welfare as the paramount consideration, directed by the statutory checklist insofar as appropriate.

KEY CASE ANALYSIS: *Re W (Relocation: Removal Outside Jurisdiction)* [2011] EWCA Civ 345

Background

- A couple separated in England. The mother was Australian and sought leave to return to Australia with her two children aged 8 and 12.
- There had been little contact with the father and there were concerns with his use of drugs and alcohol.
- The mother suffered post-natal depression, but her main reason was that she and the children would have a better life in Australia.
- It was accepted she would be devastated if leave was not granted. However, the judge refused to grant leave because of the impact on the child's relationship with the father.

Principle established

The Court of Appeal held that the judge had given too little weight to the mother's well-being and the impact on her of a refusal to leave.

It is well established that if the resident parent does not have clear plans over where the child will be educated or live in the new country leave will not be granted (*Re F (Leave to Remove)* [2005]). It seems that the courts are particularly sympathetic to parents who are seeking to return to their own country where they will have a network of friends and family to help them raise the child.

KEY CASE ANALYSIS: *K v K (Relocation: Shared care Arrangement)* [2011] EWCA Civ 793

Background

- On separation the care of two children aged 4 and 2 was shared between the parents. Each fortnight the children spent six days with the father followed by eight days with the mother.
- The mother wished to relocate to Canada.
- The judge had purported to follow the Payne guidance and held that the mother had reasonable proposals to relocate.

Principle established

- The Court of Appeal said that the only principle of general application from Payne was that the welfare principle was the guiding rule.
- The fact this case involved a shared care case was an important factor to take into account.

FIERCE DEBATE

The approach to relocation has proved fierce debate. Some argue that the courts have failed to take adequate account of the rights of children to contact. Others argue that the courts must protect the rights of freedom of movement of mothers. Some are impressed by the court's recognition of the importance of the resident parent's welfare as a part of the welfare of the child: the interests of the two are closely connected. Others say that this overlooks the importance to the child of their ties with their friends and relations in the UK.

SECTION 91(14) ORDERS

A section 91(14) order allows the court to state that an applicant cannot make any further applications in relation to the particular child without the permission of the court. It is used in cases where it is feared an applicant will make repeated, unnecessary and disruptive applications to court. In particular, in a case where the other parent will be required repeatedly to turn up to court to defend spurious applications, which will harm the resident parent and the child.

It is significant that this is not an absolute bar from accessing the court. That would probably breach Article 6 of the ECHR. Rather it requires leave to be obtained first. The court will refuse leave it if is thought that the application has no merit, but is free to give leave if it believes a genuine issue has been raised.

The courts have generally been reluctant to make the order.

KEY CASE ANALYSIS: *Re P (Section 91(14) Guidelines)*

Background

A mother sought a section 91(14) order against the father, fearing he would bring court proceedings to disrupt her parenting.

Principle established

- A section 91(14) order should only be made if it would be in the welfare of the child.
- The power is to be used with "great care and sparingly" and only as a weapon of last resort.
- It is appropriate were there have been repeated and unreasonable applications.
- It can be imposed without limit of time, although normally it should be limited.

SUMMARY

- Children do have human rights, but they are limited if a child needs capacity to exercise them.
- Disputes over children are resolved by application of the welfare principle.
- The courts have tended to reject presumptions and preferred to focus on the welfare of the child in a particular case.

FURTHER READING

B Fehlberg, "Legislating for shared parenting: How the Family Justice Review got it right" (2012) *Family Law* 709 – looks at whether there should be a presumption in favour of shared residence.

R George, "Reviewing relocation?" (2012) *Child and Family Law Quarterly* 108 – an examination of the law on relocation.

S Gilmore, "Disputing contact: Challenging some assumption" (2008) *Child and Family Law Quarterly* 285 – considers the law on contact.

J Herring and R Taylor, "Relocating relocation" (2006) *Child and Family Law Quarterly* 517 – a critical discussion of the law on relocation.

F Kaganas, "Regulating emotion: Judging contact disputes" (2011) *Child and Family Law Quarterly* 63 – examines the law on contact.

H Reece, "UK women's groups' child contact campaign 'so long as it is safe'" (2006) *Child and Family Law Quarterly* 538 – looks at feminist responses to contact disputes.

H Rhoades, "Legislating to promote children's welfare and the quest for certainty" (2012) *Child and Family Law Quarterly* 158 – considers the role of the welfare principle.

Chapter 9
Child abuse

LEARNING OBJECTIVES

After reading this chapter you should be able to:

- know what orders are available to protect children from abuse;
- understand what needs to be shown before a care order can be made;
- be able to state the effects of a care order.

INTRODUCTION

The removal of a child from her parents is one of the most dramatic orders that a court can make. Who would want to be a judge hearing cases where social workers allege a child is being seriously abused, but the parents fiercely deny it? Remove the child and you might be destroying a perfectly innocent family's life. Leave the child and you might be abandoning the child to abuse. The history of child protection has plenty of cases where children have not been protected from abuse and cases where children have been unnecessarily removed.

REAL WORLD

The NSPCC (a children's charity) claims that one in four young adults has been mistreated during childhood. It notes that the popular misconception is that children are primarily abused by strangers, whereas in fact over half of abuse is committed by parents or guardians. 11.5 per cent of young adults have experienced severe physical violence during childhood and 24.1 per cent have suffered sexal abuse.

KEY DUTIES ON A LOCAL AUTHORITY

Part III of the Children Act 1989 imposes a set of duties on local authorities. These are designed to prevent cases of child abuse occurring. For example, section 17 requires local authorities to provide services to children in need in their area. This might range from practical help, such as breakfast clubs at schools, to advice for parents who are struggling. Section 20 creates a specific duty to provide accommodation for children in need. This is designed to avoid children becoming homeless.

Key definition: the general duty

The Children Act 1989, section 17(1) states:

It shall be the general duty of every local authority (in addition to the other duties imposed on them by this Part)–

(a)   to safeguard and promote the welfare of children within their area who are in need; and

(b)   so far as is consistent with that duty, to promote the upbringing of such children by their families,

by providing a range and level of services appropriate to those children's needs.

At first sight the general duty in section 17 looks like an important section. However as the following decision makes clear it is not enforceable in court, save in exceptional cases, and so whatever its political or symbolic significance, its practical importance is limited.

KEY CASE ANALYSIS: *R(G) v Barnet LBC* [2003] UKHL 57

Background

In a set of cases heard together parents argued that under section 17 particular services should be offered to their children who were in need. Several cases were taken to the House of Lords.

Principle established

Section 17 sets out duties of a general character that are intended for all children in the need in the area of the local social services. They do not create a claim for a particular child.

Key definition: suitable accommodation

Section 20 of the Children Act 1989 states:

1   Every local authority shall provide accommodation for any child in need within their area who appears to them to require accommodation as a result of–

   (a)   there being no person who has parental responsibility for him;

   (b)   his being lost or having been abandoned; or

   (c)   the person who has been caring for him being prevented (whether or not permanently, and for whatever reason) from providing him with suitable accommodation or care.

Accommodation must be provided if the child's welfare is likely to be seriously prejudiced without it and the child is aged between 16 and 18.

Notable under s 20(6) the local authority must take into account the child's wishes and feelings and give them due regard. Accommodation is commonly provided by placing the child with a relative, host family or in a children's home.

There is no duty on a local authority to provide accommodation if a person with parental responsibility objects and is able to provide accommodation themselves (s 20(7)). If the local authority has concerns about the way the person with parental responsibility will care for the child then they must seek a care order. These provisions are designed to prevent the provision of accommodation being used as a back door means of a care order. That said, it is not difficult to imagine some cases where the local authority offers accommodation, but the parent does not object because they realise that if they do the local authority may well apply for a care order and remove the child with force.

CARE ORDER

> ### Key definition: care order
>
> When a care order is made the local authority has a duty to receive the child into their care and keep them in their care. The local authority gains parental responsibility for the child and can determine how the parents can exercise their parental responsibility. In practical terms this means that the local authority can remove a child from her parents and arrange alternative care.

Only a local authority or the NSPCC can apply for a care order. To obtain a care order the local authority has to show two things:

1   the "**threshold criteria**" have been met; and
2   it would be in the welfare of the child for the care order to be made.

Notice that it is crucial the local authority applies for a care order and establishes the threshold criteria. It cannot simply remove a child because it thinks that is suitable.

KEY CASE ANALYSIS: *R (G) V Nottingham CC* [2008] EWHC 142 (Admin)

Background

- A child was removed just two days after birth.
- The mother was 18, had been in care and had a history of alcohol and drug abuse.
- The social workers were convinced the mother posed a serious risk to the child.

Principle established

- Munby J ordered the immediate return to the mother.
- A child cannot be removed from a parent without judicial authorisation.
- The only exception to that principle was where there was a risk of immediate violence towards the child and that was not the case here.

The threshold criteria

Key definition: threshold criteria

The threshold criteria is defined in section 31 of the Children Act 1989 as follows:

(a) that the child concerned is suffering, or is likely to suffer, significant harm; and

(b) that the harm, or likelihood of harm, is attributable to –

(i) the care given to the child, or likely to be given to him if the order were not made, not being what it would be reasonable to expect a parent to give to him; or

(ii) the child's being beyond parental control.

There are several things to notice about the threshold criteria. First it has to be shown that the child either is suffering significant harm or is likely to in the future. This means that it is possible for a care order to be made even if the child has not yet suffered any harm. That said, it is highly unlikely that a court would be persuaded that there was a sufficient risk of significant harm, unless there was some strong evidence of that.

Second, the word harm is interpreted broadly. It includes ill-treatment or impairment of health or development. Development includes physical, intellectual, emotional social or behavioural development. Clearly serious physical or sexual abuse is covered. So too is neglect. Harm can be caused by omissions as well as acts.

Third, when deciding whether there is harm the child must be compared with a similar child of the same intellectual and social situation (*Re O (A Minor) (Care Proceedings: Education)* [1992]). This requirement is in place because it would be wrong if a disabled child was said to be suffering as she was performing less well than her contemporaries, but was receiving excellent care from her parents.

Fourth, it must be shown that the harm or risk of harm is caused by the parental care. The courts have recognised that there are a range of parenting styles used and that is generally a good thing. Not every parent can be perfect. Some parents will be good at some parental tasks and others good at others. This means that just because a parent is behaving in a substandard way does not meant that the threshold criteria have been met. It must be shown that the level of care is sufficiently well below the standard expected that the law must intervene.

Fifth, the phrase "likely" to suffer harm has been interpreted to mean "a real possibility that harm would be suffered". That does not mean it must be shown more likely than not that there will be significant harm, but that there is more than a faint possibility (*Re B (A Child)* 2013). However, and here admittedly it gets a little confusing, the finding of a risk must be based on facts, which need to be proved on the balance of probability (i.e. as more likely than not to be true).

FIERCE DEBATE

Imagine a case where it is alleged a step-father touched his daughter sexually in her bedroom. The matter is investigated and the evidence suggests that the event might have happened, but it has not been proved as more likely than not as having happened. In short, we just don't know. Then, it seems a care order has not been proved as there is no "fact" proved upon which to make the order. Contrast a case where it is proved the step-father viewed child pornography. This is a proven fact and might be used as the basis for a care order on the basis that it demonstrates there is a real possibility he might cause his daughter significant harm later.

This approach is highly controversial. Imagine a case where there are lots of suspicious circumstances, but no one fact proved beyond reasonable doubt. Some commentators believe a large number of suspicious circumstances can make a convincing case. Others (including the courts, most recently in *Re J (Children)* [2013]) think a child should not be removed from parents based simply on suspicions.

KEY CASE ANALYSIS: *Re H (Minors) (Sexual Abuse: Standard of Proof)* [1996] AC 563 (HL)

Background

- Three girls alleged they had been abused by their mother's cohabitant.
- He was charged with sexual offence, but acquitted at a trial.
- The local authority sought a care order in respect of the children.

Principle established

- The burden of proof for demonstrating that the threshold criteria had been met fell on those seeking the care order.
- The court could only find the threshold criteria established on the basis of facts proved on the balance of probabilities.
- The court will not rely on suspicions. Where a serious allegation was made it was harder to show on the balance of probabilities that the allegation was true.
- Where it was claimed that it was likely a child would suffer significant harm then the word likely was to mean that there was a real possibility of significant harm. That did not require proof that it was more likely than not that the child would suffer significant harm, just that it was a real possibility.

FIERCE DEBATE

One particular passage in *Re H* has caused difficulties. This was the suggestion that it was harder to prove more serious allegations than less serious allegations. Understandably that produced an outcry in that it seems to imply it would be harder to protect children in cases where the abuse was most serious. However, later cases have made it clear that that was not what their lordships meant. In *Re S-B (Children)* [2009] the House of Lords made it clear that the basic rule is that the facts must be proved on the balance of probability. However, where a very serious allegation is made that may be harder to prove on the balance of probabilities. The argument seems to be that extreme abuse cases are rarely and hence less likely to be true. Fortunately Baroness Hale in *Re B* has clarified the issue by saying that all their lordships meant is that the inherent unlikelihood of an allegation was a factor in deciding whether it had been proved to be true or not.

KEY CASE ANALYSIS: *Re B (Children) (Sexual Abuse: Standard of Proof)* **[2008] UKHL 35**

Background

- The case concerned two children aged 6 and 9 and their parents Mr and Mrs B. Mrs B had two older children by a previous marriage.
- One of the older girls (R) alleged that Mr B had abused her. Care proceedings were brought in respect of the younger children on the basis that if Mr B had abused one of the older girls he might abuse one of the younger girls too.
- Various allegations were made by R, some of which by the time of the hearing were found to be untrue.
- At the trial Charles J said he could not find that Mr B had abused R. Although he could not rule it out, it would just be a guess whether there was abuse or not. All he was prepared to say was that he could not say there was not possibility that Mr B had abused R.

Principle established

- The courts had to prove the threshold criteria on the balance of probabilities.
- It was wrong to suggest that the more serious the allegation the more proof is required.

Baroness Hale said:

> I wish to announce loud and clear that the standard of proof in finding the facts necessary to establish the threshold under s 31 (2) or the welfare consideration in section 1 of the1989 Act is the simple balance of probabilities, neither more nor less. Neither the seriousness of the allegations nor the seriousness of the consequences should make any difference to the standard of proof to be applied in determining the facts. The inherent probabilities are simply something to be taken into account, where relevant, in deciding where the truth lies.

Applying this to the facts of the case, the abuse of the older girl by Mr B had not been proved on the facts and so there were no facts that could be relied upon to establish the grounds.

Although this sounds a relatively clear decision in *Re S-B* [2009] the House of Lords were again required to make it clear that all facts had to be proved on the balance of probability. The severity of the allegation did not impact on the balance of probability. However, the inherent unlikeliness of the allegation (e.g. if it was particularly bizarre could be a factor).

KEY CASE ANALYSIS: *Lancashire CC v B* **[2000] 1 FLR 583**

Background

- Baby A had been shaken and suffered harm. It was not possible to work out who had done the shaking. It may have been A's parents or the childminder.
- The childminder had a child B. Care proceedings were brought in relation to child A and B.
- The Court of Appeal refused to make a care order for child B because it had not been shown that the childminder caused the harm and so B was at risk of harm.
- However a care order could be made in relation to A because someone caring for the child had caused the harm.

Principle established

- The threshold criteria had been met in relation to child A. Child A had suffered significant harm. That was attributable to "the care given to the child".
- It did not need to be shown which of the child's primary carers (the parents or childminder) had harmed the child as long it was a carer.

It is important to realise some of the limitations of this decision. First, it was a case where it was clear that the child had been harmed by one of three people (the parents or childminder) all of whom were involved in the child's care. The threshold criteria could not be used if it was possible the person who had harmed the child was not a carer. That is why the threshold criteria were not met in relation to B.

Second, their lordships were simply finding that the threshold criteria were satisfied. In a case like this it was possible that the court would decide not to make an order, or that a supervision order was possible. The court would need to consider what order to make on the basis that the parents were possible perpetrators (*Re O and N* [2003]).

Third, an issue not raised in these cases, was whether in some cases where a stranger has harmed the child, the parent might be blamed on the basis of failing to ensure that the child was endangered by the behaviour of others. In such a case the threshold criteria could be made out.

Cases where it is clear the child has been abused but it is not clear who has committed the abuse are known as "unknown perpetrator" cases.

KEY CASE ANALYSIS: *Re S-B* [2009] UKSC 17

Background

- A baby was bruised and harmed but it was unclear if the mother or father had caused the harm.
- The mother left the father and set up home with a new partner and had children.
- The local authority sought a care order in relation to the new children on the basis she may have harmed the past child.

Principle established

It was held that it had not been shown on the facts that she had harmed the child. She was a possible perpetrator but this was not a factor that could be relied upon because it had not been proved on the balance of probabilities that she had harmed the child.

Note that in relation to the first child the threshold criteria had been met. It had been shown that the child had been harmed by someone caring for her. But in relation to the new children it had not been shown that the mother posed a risk to the children.

The welfare stage

It is very important to appreciate that a care order should not be made simply because the threshold criteria have been met. It is common for the threshold criteria to be met but the court to decide that a care order is not in the welfare or the child. A key factor in deciding whether or not to make a care order at the welfare stage is that of proportionality.

Key definition: proportionality

The court must ensure that the extent of intervention in the life of the child and her family is proportionate to the risk faced by the child. The removal of a child will only be proportionate if it is the least intrusive measure into family life that will appropriately protect the child. In particular the court must consider whether a supervision order will be more appropriate as a way of protecting the child.

KEY CASE ANALYSIS: *Re C and B (Care Order: Future Harm)* [2001] FLR 611

Background

- There were concerns about the care of two children.
- The local authority removed the children and did not allow any contact between the children and parents.

Principle established

- Any intervention to protect children had to be necessary and proportionate.
- Here severing all contact between a child and their family required strong evidence based on the welfare of the child.

KEY CASE ANALYSIS: *Re S (A Child) (Care and Placement Orders: Proportionality)* [2013] EWCA Civ 1073

Background

- A mother with learning disabilities who was living in supported accommodation gave birth to a child (K).
- The local authority started care proceedings.
- The judge found that the mother could not care for K in the community although she had being doing well in the supportive accommodation.

- The judge made a care order and a placement order (with a view to adoption).

Principle established

- The mother's appeal was allowed.
- A care order and placement order were "extreme" and should only be made when all else had failed.
- It was in a child's best interests to be brought up her natural parents and adoption was a last resort.
- The orders were not proportionate to the risk facing the child.

The wishes of the child can be a relevant factor in deciding what order to make. The courts will tread carefully here and want an expert report. One of the effects of the abuse can be to produce a strong attachment between the victim and the abuser. However, the older and more mature the child the greater the weight that might be attached to her views. The views of a child who strongly wanted to be removed from her parents are particularly likely to be taken seriously.

KEY CASE ANALYSIS: *Re H (Care Order: Contact)* [2008] EWCA Civ 1245

Background

- A care order was made in relation to a ten-year-old girl.
- She was very keen to remain with her mother and had a strong relationship with her.

Principle established

- The Court of Appeal replaced the care order with a residence order and a supervision order.
- The strong wishes of a mature child were to be taken into account. The relationship between mother and daughter in this case was important to her well-being.

The effect of a care order

A care order gives parental responsibilities to the local authority. The parents retain parental responsibility, but the local authority can decide to what extent the parents can exercise their parental responsibilities. The court is not permitted to put restrictions on what happens once a care order is made. The local authority will decide where the child should live and make decisions about the child's day-to-day life. The court therefore, has a "gatekeeper role" and decides whether or not a care order is made, but not what happens thereafter. This can be troubling. A court may make a care order on the basis of the care plan submitted by the local authority (e.g. that it will leave the child with the parents but supply parenting classes and support) but once the care order is made the local authority might decide to do something completely different (e.g. remove the child from the parents). The argument in favour of the approach taken by the courts is that it means the local authority can respond quickly to changing events rather than seeking court approval each time there is a change in the circumstances. It is also arguable that the local authority and the social workers involved in the case know the child best and need the flexibility and speed of being able to make decisions themselves. Perhaps most significantly there is the issue of money. Local authorities have limited resources to spend on children in their care. They have the difficult job of deciding how to balance the competing claims of a range of children. That is difficult for a court to do.

Where a care order has been made there is a duty on the local authority to allow reasonable contact with parents.

Key definition: contact with children in care

Section 34 of the Children Act 1989 states:

(1) Where a child is in the care of a local authority, the authority shall (subject to the provisions of this section) allow the child reasonable contact with–

    (a) his parents;

    (b) any guardian or special guardian of his;

    (ba) any person who by virtue of section 4A has parental responsibility for him;

    (c) where there was a residence order in force with respect to the child immediately before the care order was made, the person in whose favour the order was made; and

    (d) where, immediately before the care order was made, a person had care of the child by virtue of an order made in the exercise of the High Court's inherent jurisdiction with respect to children, that person . . .

The local authority can, in the case of an emergency refuse contact for up to seven days (s 34(6)) but if a longer period is required then a court order is required. The court will apply the welfare principle in section 1 of the Children Act 1989 in deciding whether to allow termination of contact.

SUPERVISION ORDER

Key definition: supervision order

The Children Act 1989 s 35(1) defines a supervision order as follows:

While a supervision order is in force it shall be the duty of the supervisor –

(a)   To advise, assist and befriend the supervised child;

(b)   To take such steps as are reasonably necessary to give effect to the order; and

(c)   Where-

(i)   The order is not wholly complied with; or

(ii)   The supervisor considers that the order may no longer be necessary,

to consider whether or not to apply to the court for its variation or discharge.

It is interesting that the supervision order puts obligations on the supervisor: to advise and assist the child. It imposes no obligations on the parents as such. However, it should be remembered that if the parents do not positively interact with the supervisor there is a real risk that a care order will be sought.

A supervision order does not give the local authority parental responsibility. That is a crucial difference from a care order, where the local authority is given parental responsibility. This means that the local authority under a supervision order has no power to make decisions in relation to, for example, education or health. The supervision order appoints an officer to assist and befriend the child. The aim is in the nature of ensuring that someone keeps an eye on the child and can give advice on what to do.

CHILD ASSESSMENT ORDER

> **Key definition: child assessment orders**
>
> The Children Act 1989, section 43 states:
>
> 1   On the application of a local authority or authorised person for an order to be made under this section with respect to a child, the court may make the order if, but only if, it is satisfied that–
>
>   (a)   the applicant has reasonable cause to suspect that the child is suffering, or is likely to suffer, significant harm;
>   (b)   an assessment of the state of the child's health or development, or of the way in which he has been treated, is required to enable the applicant to determine whether or not the child is suffering, or is likely to suffer, slificant harm; and
>   (c)   it is unlikely that such an assessment will be made, or be satisfactory, in the absence of an order under this section.

The child assessment order is designed to enable a medical or psychiatric assessment of the child to take place. This might provide evidence to assist in determining whether the threshold criteria are made out. The child assessment order is, therefore, not appropriate in a case where a child needs immediate protection, but rather that further investigations are needed. In fact the child assessment order is rarely used.

EMERGENCY PROTECTION ORDER

> **Key definition: emergency protection order**
>
> The Children Act 1989, section 44 states:
>
> 1   Where any person ("the applicant") applies to the court for an order to be made under this section with respect to a child, the court may make the order if, but only if, it is satisfied that–

(a)   there is reasonable cause to believe that the child is likely to suffer significant harm if–

(i)   he is not removed to accommodation provided by or on behalf of the applicant; or

(ii)   he does not remain in the place in which he is then being accommodated;

(b)   in the case of an application made by a local authority–

(i)   enquiries are being made with respect to the child under s 47(1)(b); and

(ii)   those enquiries are being frustrated by access to the child being unreasonably refused to a person authorised to seek access and that the applicant has reasonable cause to believe that access to the child is required as a matter of urgency; or

(c)   in the case of an application made by an authorised person–

(i)   the applicant has reasonable cause to suspect that a child is suffering, or is likely to suffer, significant harm;

(ii)   the applicant is making enquiries with respect to the child's welfare; and

(iii)   those enquiries are being frustrated by access to the child being unreasonably refused to a person authorised to seek access and the applicant has reasonable cause to believe that access to the child is required as a matter of urgency.

The emergency protection order is appropriate where there is an emergency and immediate intervention is needed. Although anyone can apply for an emergency protection order, in fact it tends to be local authorities who do so. Indeed if a local authority has decided not to apply for an emergency protection order it is hard to believe the court will make one.

As can be seen from the definition above the court will require proof that there is reasonable cause to believe that the child is likely to suffer significant harm if she is not removed to accommodation or remain in accommodation.

The courts have accepted that an EPO is a harsh measure and there must be "extraordinarily compelling reasons". It must be shown there is an imminent danger (*Re M (Care Proceedings: Judicial Review)* [2003]). If an emergency protection order is made it must last for as short a time as possible. Normally a local authority will quickly prepare to make an application for a care order.

KEY CASE ANALYSIS: *X Council v B (Emergency Protection Orders)* **[2004] EWHC 2014 (Fam)**

Background

- Children were taken into foster care following *ex parte* emergency protection orders.
- There were concerns about the children's well-being.

Principle established

- Proportionality was a key factor.
- It was accepted by Munby J that intervention was justified. However removal of the children and severe limitations on contact were not necessary.
- There was a need for medical tests and examinations. These could be done without an emergency protection order.

SUMMARY

- The local authority has a general duty to provide services and accommodation to children in need in its area.
- A care or supervision order can be made if it is shown that the child is suffering or is likely to suffer significant harm as a result of the parenting he or she has received and that it would be in the welfare of the child to make such an order.
- Once a care order has been made the local authority acquires parental responsibility for the child and can remove them.
- Emergency protection orders can be made in urgent cases.

FURTHER READING

R Bailey Harris and J Harris, "Local authorities and child protection: The mosaic of accountability" (2002) *Child and Family Law Quarterly* 117 – looks at accountability in child abuse law.

J Hayes, M Hayes and C Williams, "Shocking abuse followed by 'staggering ruling'" (2010) *Family Law* 166 – considers some controversial decisions on child abuse.

H Keating, "The significance of harm" (2011) *Child and Family Law Quarterly* 115 – looks at the threshold criteria.

J Mason, "Reforming care proceedings: Time for review" (2007) *Child and Family Law Quarterly* 411 – discusses whether we need to reform the law on care orders.

Chapter 10
Adoption

LEARNING OBJECTIVES

After reading this chapter you should be able to:

- understand the nature of adoption;
- be able to explain the grounds upon which an adoption order can be made;
- explain the nature and purpose of special guardianship.

INTRODUCTION

If a child can no longer live with their parents, the state has a duty to ensure the child receives good alternative care. A popular way of doing that is to arrange for the child to be **adopted**. This means another parent or parents take over the role of caring for that child.

There is considerable public debate over adoption. This chapter considers when adoption is used and what must be proved before a court will make an adoption order. It will also look at the relatively recent status of **special guardianship** and the role that plays in child protection.

REAL WORLD

Adoption is, in fact, not common. In 2013 only 4,000 children were placed for adoption, out of 68,000 children in care. The Government has said it wants to greatly increase the rates of adoption. While traditionally it was babies who were primarily put up for adoption, now it is most commonly children who have been removed from their parents following abuse.

There has been a notable drop in the number of adoptions over the past few decades. In 1971 there were 21,495 adoptions. There were 5,206 adoptions entered into the Adopted Children Register (ACR) following court orders made in England (4,835) and Wales (371) during 2012:

- 2 per cent of children adopted during the year ending 31 March 2013 were under 1 year old.
- 74 per cent (2,960) were aged between 1 and 4 years old.
- 21 per cent (850) were aged between 5 and 9 years old.
- 2 per cent (70) were aged between 10 and 15 years old.
- <1 per cent (10) were aged 16 and over.

WHO CAN ADOPT?

At one time only married couples could adopt. The 2002 Adoption and Children Act expanded the list of who can apply to include:

- married couples
- civil partners
- cohabiting couples (whether opposite or same-sex couples)
- single people.

One of the few restrictions is that an adopter must be over the age of 21.

The argument that was used to justify the extension of who can adopt was that the adoption agency should be encouraged to find the right match between the child and the adopters. Allowing a broad range of adopters increased the chance a good match will be found.

WHO CAN BE ADOPTED?

Only children under the age of 18 can be adopted. As we saw in the "real world" box above, it is now relatively rare for babies to be adopted. In the past adoption was used especially by unmarried mothers who felt it was unsuitable for them to raise an "illegitimate" child. Now, it tends to be slightly older children who have suffered abuse or neglect who are put up for adoption.

THE ADOPTION PROCEDURE

The adoption procedure is made up of five steps as follows:

1   The adoption agency determines that adoption is appropriate for the child. Significantly this will mean the agency has decided that the long-term future of the child does not lie with her parents.

2   The adoption agency will assess people who come forward wanting to adopt children and assess whether they are compatible or not.

3   The agency will determine which of the approved adopters is most suitable for the particular child. This is known as "matching".

4   Placement. Usually the local authority seeks a court order authorising that the child live with the potential adopters for a trial period. Before a placement order can be made the court will need to be persuaded that the threshold criteria (see Chapter 9) are made out; the order is in the welfare of the child; and the parents have consented or the consent of the parents has been dispensed with. Sometimes the birth parents will agree to the placement in which case no order is needed.

5   The court makes the adoption order and it is finalised.

When the court makes an adoption order or a placement order there are two questions. Is the order in the welfare of the child? Has the birth parent consented or has the need for their consent been dispensed with?

The welfare of the child

The adoption agency and the court in their decisions must ensure that the "child's welfare throughout his life" (Adoption and Children Act 2002, s 1(2)) is their paramount consideration. This is explained further in s 1(4).

Key definition: welfare of the child

The Children Act 1989, section 1(3) states that the following factors should be taken into account when the welfare of the child is considered in adoption decisions:

(a) the child's ascertainable wishes and feelings regarding the decision (considered in the light of the child's age and understanding),

(b) the child's particular needs,

(c) the likely effect on the child (throughout his life) of having ceased to be a member of the original family and become an adopted person,

(d) the child's age, sex, background and any of the child's characteristics which the court or agency considers relevant,

(e)   any harm (within the meaning of the Children Act 1989) which the
      child has suffered or is at risk of suffering,

(f)   the relationship which the child has with relatives, and with any other
      person in relation to whom the court or agency considers the
      relationship to be relevant including–

      (i)   the likelihood of any such relationship continuing and the value to
             the child of its doing so,

      (ii)   the ability and willingness of any of the child's relatives, or of any
             such person, to provide the child with a secure environment in
             which the child can develop, and otherwise to meet the child's
             needs,

      (iii) the wishes and feelings of any of the child's relatives, or of any
             such person, regarding the child.

It is worth adding that under s 1(3) the "court or adoption agency must at all times bear in mind that, in general, any delay in coming to the decision is likely to prejudice the child's welfare".

Another important factor is that "the adoption agency must give due consideration to the child's religious persuasion, racial origins and cultural and linguistic background" (s 1(5)) when determining placement decisions. However, it should be remembered that this factor is only one of many. In *Re S* [2005] the court was reluctant to delay a placement so that an adopter of the same religion as the child could be found.

One factor in the above list to particularly take account of is the importance of any relatives in the life of the child. If a child cannot be cared for by his parents the local authority are likely to consider care by other family members before turning to the possibility of adoption. Of course, there is nothing to stop a child being adopted by a family member, but special guardianship (see below) or a more informal arrangement may be appropriate if a relative is to take on the care of a child.

Parental consent

An adoption order terminates the parental status of the birth parents. It is, therefore, hugely significant for them. This means that before an adoption or placement order can be made either the birth parents need to consent or the court must determine that the consent of the birth parents is not needed.

Key definition: consent to adoption

Consent must be given unconditionally and with full understanding of what adoption means. A person can consent to adoption either to a specific person or to adoption by the person selected by the adoption agency and approved by the court.

In relation to a mother, consent to adoption must be given more than six weeks after the child's birth (s 52(3)). The justification for this is that we want to be sure this is the definite decision of the mother and not a decision made in the aftermath of birth. It is possible for consent to placement to be given at any time.

KEY CASE ANALYSIS: *A Local Authority v GC* **[2008] EWHC 2555 (Fam)**

Background

A mother and father consented to placement and adoption when their child was only four weeks old.

Principle established

- The mother's consent could not be regarded as valid as it was not given more than six weeks after birth.
- However, it was clearly in the child's interests for the adoption to continue and so the requirements for consent would be dispensed with.

Who needs to give consent?

Before an adoption order can be made parents, guardians or special guardians who have parental responsibility must give their consent or have that requirement dispensed with by the court. Note that the consent of an unmarried father without parental responsibility is not required. That said, the courts have used the Human Rights Act 1998 to say that an unmarried father should be informed of the proceedings and he will normally be entitled to attend and have his say, even though officially his consent is not required. The courts will have flexibility over this though.

KEY CASE ANALYSIS: *Re C* [2007] EWCA Civ 1206

Background

After a very brief relationship the mother became pregnant. She, aged 19, did not want the child's father or her parents to know about the birth. She wished to have the child adopted.

Principle established

- The Court of Appeal directed that the father should not be notified to see if he was in a position to offer long-term care of the child.
- It was argued that not informing the father would breach his Article 8 rights, but as he had no established relationship with the child or mother he had no right to respect of his family life in relation to the child.
- Interestingly the court thought that the grandparents did have the right to be informed as they had rights under Article 8.

Dispensing with consent

If a person with parental responsibility refuses to consent or they cannot be found then the court must dispense with the consent requirement. The criteria for doing this are set out in s 52(1) of the Adoption and Children Act 2002.

Key definition: dispensing with consent

1   The court cannot dispense with the consent of any parent or guardian of a child to the child being placed for adoption or to the making of an adoption order in respect of the child unless the court is satisfied that–

   (a) the parent or guardian cannot be found or is incapable of giving consent, or
   (b) the welfare of the child requires the consent to be dispensed with.

There are two grounds for dispensing with consent. The first is where the parent cannot provide the consent because they lack the capacity to do so or cannot be found. The second is more controversial. Notice it is not enough just to show that it would be in the welfare of the child to dispense with consent. Rather it must be shown the welfare *requires* the consent to be dispensed with. Notably the courts will also take into account the Human Rights Act 1998 and the European Court of Human Rights has made it clear that adoption usually involves a breach of the rights of the parents and child and there needs to be sufficient justification for that breach. That implies that if the case is borderline, i.e. the adoption will be very slightly in the welfare of the child, this might not be sufficient to shown that dispensing with consent is required (*Re Q (A Child)* [2011]).

As already mentioned, one issue that the courts will take into account is the European Convention of Human Rights. The European Court has taken the view that adoption, with its severing of the relationship between the birth parent and the child, requires exceptional circumstances to be justified.

KEY CASE ANALYSIS: *Johansen v Norway* **[1997] 23 EHRR 33**

Background

The child had been removed from the mother and placed with a view for adoption.

Principle established

- "The mutual enjoyment by parent and child of each other's company constitutes a fundamental element of family life and domestic measures hindering such enjoyment mount to an interference with the right protected by Article 8" (*Johansen v Norway* [1997] EHRR 33, 65).
- Only exceptional circumstances could justify the interference in the Article 8 rights of parents and children caused by an adoption.

The European Court has made it clear that it is not saying that an adoption can never be justified, but it is clear that it will require strong reasons.

THE EFFECT OF PLACEMENT

If a placement order is made then parental responsibility is given to the local authority. If the child is placed with prospective adopters then parental responsibility is given to them as well. Importantly during the placement the birth parents do not lose their parental responsibility nor their parental status. However, these will be extinguished once the final adoption order is made.

During a placement the parental responsibility will be shared between the adoption agency and the adopters. In the case of any dispute the agency has to determine the extent to which parental responsibility is exercised. It also ultimately has the power to remove the child from the potential adopters if necessary. However, only the local authority can remove the child. Of course, the birth parent cannot. While the child is being placed it is not possible to change the surname of the child or remove the child from the UK, except for short holidays. It is possible to get the permission of the court to do this.

REVOCATION OF A PLACEMENT

Under section 24 of the Adoption and Children Act 2002 any person can apply to revoke the placement order, except the child and local authority, if a leave is given by the court. However, leave will only be granted if there has been a change of circumstances since the placement order has been made. The law here is seeking to strike a balance. Once the court has determined that it is in the welfare of the child to have the child placed and the issue of parental consent has been dealt with, it wants the child's placement to proceed peacefully. Allowing a birth parent to keep challenging the placement would undermine the stability of the placement and might, in effect, give birth parents a second bite at the cherry. On the other hand there is acknowledgment that there can be cases where a placement has been agreed on the basis of certain facts but it has become clear that these have changed and the child should be returned to the parents.

When deciding whether to give leave to allow an application to revoke the placement the welfare of the child is not the paramount consideration but is a relevant consideration. Clearly a key requirement is that there has been a change of circumstances. The court will also consider whether there is a real prospect of the application to revoke succeeding. The court will also consider the delay that granting leave will cause to the adoption process and the impact of that on the child (*Re A: Coventry County Council v CC and A* [2007]).

The case law makes it clear that leave will not be granted simply because it has been shown there is a change of circumstances. For example in *M v Warwickshire County Council* [2007] the Court of Appeal accepted that there was a change of circumstances in that the mother had abstained from drugs, reduced her alcohol consumption to a reasonable level and attended an HIV clinic. Nevertheless bearing in mind the welfare of the child it was best not to allow leave to revoke the placement order.

One factor that might particularly influence the court in allowing leave is if there is evidence that the child is not doing well in the placement. In *NS-H v Kingston Upon Hull City Council* [2008] the Court of Appeal allowed the mother leave to apply to revoke the placement. The child had not been thriving in foster care and not been developing well generally. This was treated as a change of circumstances, which made it appropriate to hear the application to revoke the placement.

The following cases discuss when a person can apply for revocation of a placement.

KEY CASE ANALYSIS: *Re G (A Child) (Leave to Apply for Residence Order: Non-Relative)* [2014] EWCA Civ 432

Background

- A mother handed her child (G) to her partner's mother (R), shortly after G's birth. The mother was unable to care for G.
- R cared for G but there were care proceedings and G was removed from R and placed with prospective adopters who later applied to adopt G.
- R sought leave to oppose the adoption. She claimed that there had been a change in her circumstances and she was now in a good position to care for G.
- Section 47 of the Children Act 1989 appeared to state that a formal application to oppose adoption could only be made by a parent or guardian and so R was not allowed to challenge the adoption.

Principle established

- The Court of Appeal held that under s 29(4) of the Children Act 1989, R could seek a residence order and that in effect would operate as a challenge to the proposed adoption.
- Leave would need to be granted and the welfare of the child was not a paramount consideration in deciding whether to give leave (although the welfare principle did apply to the actual decision of the residence order).
- On the facts of the case there was no realistic chance of success for R's application and it would not be appropriate to grant leave.

KEY CASE ANALYSIS: *Re L (A Child) (Leave to Oppose Making of Adoption Order)* **[2013] EWCA Civ 1481**

Background

- A mother gave birth to S when she was 15. It was held that the mother lacked some basic parenting skills.
- The child was placed with Mr and Mrs X with a view to adoption. They subsequently applied for adoption and the mother opposed.
- Mr and Mrs X had adopted a child previously but had separated and divorce proceedings had been commenced. Mrs X wanted to play no part in S's adoption and the proposal was that S would live with Mr X and his new partner (who was expecting Mr X's baby). They had not yet reached an agreement over Y (their adopted child).
- The local authority opposed the mother's application under s 47(5) to oppose on the basis that she still lacked the skills needed to meet S's needs. The mother responded by arguing she had a network of friends to support her.
- The judge concluded that the support network for the mother was a change in circumstances, but that the mother's chances of success were very remote as her plan lacked substance and solidity.
- While it was true that Mr (and/or Mrs) X might not succeed in their adoption application, if they failed S would be placed with other prospective adopters offering good care. That would be preferable to exposing S to the mother's care.

Principle established

- The Court of Appeal held that the judge had failed to give adequate weight to the fact that the original proposals for adoption were now unlikely to succeed and there was considerable uncertainty about S's future.
- The separation of Mr and Mrs X and uncertainty over their family situation was a significant change in circumstances. It was quite possible Mr X would not succeed in his adoption application in which case serious consideration could be given to the mother being reconsidered as the carer.
- The judge should have compared the uncertainty in the placement with the care of the mother.
- Leave to hear the mother's application should have been granted.

KEY CASE ANALYSIS: *Re D (A Child) (Leave to Oppose Making of Adoption Order)* [2013] EWCA Civ 1480

Background

- M gave birth to baby L when she was 16. A care order was made as it was found that M was failing to meet L's needs and there were concerns about her relationships with violent men.
- L was placed for adoption.
- The mother sought leave to challenge the placement after she had success in dealing with her problems with alcohol and relationships with men. The judge refused leave.

Principle established

- The questions of whether there was a change in circumstances and whether there were solid grounds for revoking the placement were intertwined.
- The picture of M was a mix of some improvement and some ongoing problems.
- It was held that the judge was entitled to decide that there was a change of circumstances, but not enough of a change to make the application likely to succeed.

THE EFFECT OF AN ADOPTION ORDER

English law on adoption uses the "transplant" model of adoption. This means that once the adoption order is made the adoptive parents take over the place of the birth parents. Then the birth parents will cease to be the parents of the child and will lose parental responsibility. The adoptive parents will become the legal parents for all purposes. This is not to say that all ties with the birth parents will necessarily be revoked. It is possible that the court will order the child to have contact with the birth parents (s 46(6)).

Once an adoption order is made, only in the most exceptional of circumstances will an adoption order be revoked.

KEY CASE ANALYSIS: *Webster v Norfolk CC* [2009] EWCA Civ 59

Background

- Mr and Mrs Webster had three children in three years. In late 2003 their middle child, B, was taken to hospital suffering multiple fractures.
- The hospital and local authority assessed the injuries to be non-accidental and caused by his parents. The children were adopted by late 2005.
- In 2006 Mrs Webster became pregnant again.
- In the course of care proceedings relating to the new baby the Websters obtained fresh expert evidence in relation to B. The new report was powerfully of the opinion that the injuries to B were caused by scurvy and iron deficiency rather than abuse. At the time scurvy was considered as unknown in the West and had not been considered as an explanation for the injuries.
- As a result the care proceedings in relation to the baby were discontinued. The parents then sought to set aside all the orders relating to their three younger children.

Principle established

- The Court of Appeal held that only in exceptional cases can an adoption order be overturned.
- There was nothing in the procedure that led to the making of the order, which rendered the procedure flawed and hence the adoption order could not be set aside.
- Wilson LJ emphasised that the children had been with the adopters for four years in an arrangement they had been told was permanent and the children were fully settled into their new life.

CONTACT AND ADOPTION

When a child is placed for adoption the agency must consider what arrangements there should be for people to have contact with the child. If a contact order under section 8 of the Children Act 1989 is in place it ceases to have effect. However, when placing a child for placement an order for contact can be made under sections 26 or 51A of the Adoption and Children Act 2002. This order would require the person with whom the child lives to allow the child to visit or stay with the other person. An order under section 51A is likely to be sought by the birth parents of the child or any relative can seek the court order. The court will apply the welfare principle in determining the order to make.

Once an adoption order is made the birth parents are no longer the parents in the eyes of the law and cease to have any right to contact. Normally adoption agencies and indeed the court persuade adoptive parents and birth families to agree informal contact arrangements between themselves if that is suitable. This is normally preferable to requiring there to be court-ordered contact. Indeed if contact with the birth parents is thought to be essential to the child's welfare this might suggest that adoption is not the ideal. Not surprisingly then it has been said by Wall LJ in *Re R (Adoption: Contact)* [2005] that it is extremely rare for there to be contact after adoption. In *Oxfordshire CC v Z, Y and J* [2010] it was held inappropriate to order the adoptive parents to send the natural parent a photograph of their child. Notably the court accepted that such an order would benefit the birth parents, but emphasised that they had to focus on what was best for the child.

ACCESS TO BIRTH RECORDS

The law recognises that once an adopted child becomes an adult they may seek to find out information about their origins. There is an adopted children register. The register can be searched on application to the Registrar General. An adopted child can generally have access to their birth certificate or information from the register, save in exceptional cases. It is worth noticing that many adopted children decide not to seek the information. However a good number do. Counselling is often offered to children who seek to obtain information.

KEY CASE ANALYSIS: *R v Registrar General ex parte Smith* [1991] 1 FLR 255

Background

A man serving a prison sentence for murder sought a copy of his birth certificate.

Principle established

This was an exceptional case where the Registrar was entitled to refuse consent. Giving him the certificate might put his birth family at risk on his release.

There is also an Adoption Contact Register that allows people to record their interests in contacting birth relatives or allows birth relatives to express an interest in contacting the adopted child. If there is a match the Registrar General gives the adopted person the information. It is left to them to decide whether they wish to make contact.

SPECIAL GUARDIANSHIP

The Adoption and Children Act 2002 created the status of special guardianship. To be able to apply automatically a person must fall into one of the following groups shown in Figure 10.1.

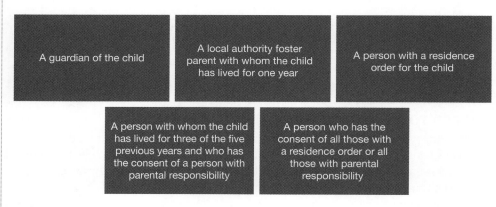

Figure 10.1 Applicants for special guardianship

If an applicant does not fall into this list they need the leave of the court before they can apply.

When deciding whether to make a special guardianship order the welfare principle will apply. The court will take account of whether a special guardianship order is more suitable for the child than an adoption order or indeed no order at all.

Special guardianship is different from adoption in several ways. Most significantly it does not bring to an end the parental status of the birth parents. Even after a special guardianship order the birth parents will remain the parents of the child. However, the special guardianship order will mean that the child will live with the special guardians. So it is suitable for a case where although the child cannot live with the parents, the parents have some role to play in the child's life. It may also be more appropriate where a family member is going to look after the child. Making, say, an aunt a parent through an adoption order may cause confusion to the child.

The differences between special guardianship and adoption are summarised in Table 10.1.

Table 10.1 The differences between adoption and special guardianship

	Adoption	Special guardianship
Parentage	The adoptive parents are the parents in the law	The birth parents remain the parents and the special guardians do not become the parents
Parental responsibility	The adoptive parents have parental responsibility. The birth parents do not	The special guardians and the birth parents have parental responsibility
Restrictions on parental responsibility	The adoptive parents have full parental responsibility	The special guardian needs the consent of the birth parents and others with PR in order to change the child's surname, remove the child from the UK for more than 3 months, and consent to adoption or medical treatment
Duration	Adoption never comes to an end	Special guardianship comes to an end when the child is 18
Intestacy	The child can inherit from adoptive parents if they die intestate	The child cannot inherit from special guardians if they die intestate
Revocation of order	Adoption order cannot be revoked save in the most exceptional circumstances (e.g. where there is a procedural impropriety)	With leave of the court, the birth parents can apply to revoke the special guardianship order if there has been a significant change of circumstances
Financial support	The birth parents can be required to provide financial support for the child	The birth parents cannot be required to provide financial support

Special guardianship, as is clear from these differences, is appropriate where it is beneficial for the child to retain a link with their birth family, but the day-to-day care of the child needs to be undertaken by someone else. When deciding whether or not to make a special guardianship order the welfare principle and the other principles apply. In addition the court must consider whether a contact order should be made and whether to vary or discharge any section 8 order.

KEY CASE ANALYSIS: *Re S (Adoption Order or Special Guardianship Order)* [2007] EWCA Civ 54

Background

- A child aged six was in care. She lived with a foster mother but the birth mother and father had regular contact.
- The foster mother wished to adopt the child but the court decided to make a special guardianship order.
- The mother appealed to the Court of Appeal.

Principle established

- The court must look at the welfare of the child and the welfare checklists before deciding whether an adoption order or special guardianship order was better. The wishes of the foster carer were a factor to consider but at the end of the day the court must focus on what is best for the child.
- The court must bear in mind Article 8 of the ECHR and ensure that any order is proportionate in its interference with the rights of family life of the birth family and the child. A special guardianship order is less of an interference than adoption and so should be used unless there are special advantages offered by adoption.
- It should be noted that special guardianship does not offer the same level of permanence as adoption. The parents can apply for a residence order without leave and so the special guardians are more at risk of having their care challenged. If the birth parents misuse their power a s 91(14) order may be appropriate.

On-the-spot question

? Do you think special guardianship is helpful? Some fear it is too insecure for adults wishing to offer long-term care for the child. They can have the child removed from them based on a welfare assessment. That said it would be surprising if a child was removed from a happy situation with a special guardian unless there were real concerns.

SUMMARY

- Adoption can be used in cases where the parents can no longer care for the child and long-term alternative parents are needed.
- On the making of an adoption order the parental status of the birth parents comes to an end and the adoptive parents become, in law, the child's parents.
- An adopted child, once they are an adult, can seek information about their birth parents.
- The court can use a special guardianship order in a case where it is helpful to retain some link with the birth family.

FURTHER READING

S Choudhry, "The Adoption and Children Act 2002, the welfare principle and the Human Rights Act 1988: A missed opportunity" (2003) *Child and Family Law Quarterly* 119 – argues the law on adoption needs to take more account of human rights.

S Hall, "Special guardianship and permanency planning: Unforeseen consequences and missed opportunities" (2008) *Child and Family Law Quarterly* 359 – examines the use of special guardianship.

S Harris-Short, "Making and breaking family life: Adoption, the state and human rights" (2008) 35 *Journal of Law and Society* 28 – a critical discussion of the law on adoption.

Index